# Change Leadership Emotional Intelligence (CLEI)

## Using Change Strategies that Work!

Cyndi Schaeffer, PhD

# About the Author

Cyndi Schaeffer, PhD, has over 20 years of experience leading high performing teams and transforming organizations. She has served as a supervisor, administrator, executive director, change manager and chief of staff. She has provided change leadership, change management, leadership development and customer service training to private and public sector companies and organizations nationally and internationally. She has been an instructor at several universities and earned her PhD from Antioch University in Leadership and Change.

# Acknowledgments

Thank you Josh McConnell, Ben and Andrew Schaeffer-McConnell for the delight of having you in my life.

Thank you Phil McConnell for your incredible and unending positive support during this journey and life.

Thank you Chuck Davis for reading the content and for your great contributions.

Thank you Bill Wells for your insightful conversations around STAMP.

Susie Debord—you are my friend, and the sister that people only dream of having.

Gail Brown—thank you for your friendship, encouragement and confidence in me.

Thank you Missy DeBord for your expert and thoughtful content proofing. Carl Cummings, you are an amazing and talented graphic artist and creator.

Thank you Tony Loton for being such a magnificent and patient editor.

To my mom and dad who always believed in me.

I am so grateful for the learning from my mentors Carol Baron, Mitch Kusy and others from Antioch University Leadership and Change PhD program.

Because of all of your support and mentorship, this book has happened.

# Foreword: Change – What's Going On?

Robert is a manager at a manufacturing company that recently has had layoffs. He has been told the company will launch a new product with new requirements and new quality standards. The current product being manufactured is no longer competitive with the international markets. The product delivery expectations are unbelievably high. Not only does Robert not know the details of this new product, he is also being asked to launch a new performance management system that requires forced ranking of company employees. The morale of his team is low, and the team is resisting the changes. Attendance is poor, morale has tanked, and the defect rate is up. Robert calls his team together and tells them to stop complaining and tells them to "get with the program or no one will have a job."

Aiguo is the executive director of a nonprofit organization. Funding has been dramatically reduced, and the organization needs to reevaluate its services, possibly eliminating some of them and expanding others. His staff is locked into the current mission and menu of services offered by the organization and is expressing concern regarding the direction the organization is taking. The organization is currently going through a building remodel, and the staff will be sitting in different parts of the building. The employees are talking about attending a board meeting and getting some one-on-one time with the board president to discuss their dissatisfaction. Aiguo is overwhelmed and tired of trying to convince his staff members they need to change their thinking. He just wants to check out.

The county director, Farhia, is pressed with a number of continual and ongoing changes. A new technology solution is being launched to track clients and case notes. Her workforce is comprised of four generations and represents numerous ethnicities and cultures. She will need to reconfigure the management team and work groups. A new political chief has been recently elected, yet there is no clarity regarding funding levels for the department or changing priorities. The staff has begun to triangulate through gossiping and many are looking for new jobs. Farhia is exhausted and unsure how to lead her department. She is tired of telling her staff about the county's new direction when it is unclear and always changing. She has stopped meeting with her management team until she gets some clear direction from upper leadership.

Matt is the dean of a local community college. The college has gone through tremendous change; the students are representing more ethnicities than ever before. Matt's primarily Caucasian instructional staff is expressing concern and frustration with the diverse student composition. Current teaching pedagogy doesn't seem to be as effective as before, and enrollment is dropping. A new college president is considering restructuring how the college does business. Matt is unhappy, worried and even angry. He has been totally transparent during a recent faculty meeting, telling the instructors that he has decided to look elsewhere for a job.

In each of the case scenarios above, the leaders lacked Change Leadership Emotional Intelligence (CLEI) and lacked the understanding and use of change management strategies. Without an understanding and use of Change Leadership Emotional Intelligence, leaders typically do not have an adequate understanding of their own feelings or skills, don't know how to control their feelings, and aren't particularly motivated. In addition to being clueless to what they are feeling or saying, they lack the ability and interest in knowing how their employees feel. They don't understand how they can support employees in moving forward to implement the change, using emotions and effective change management strategies.

# Chapter 2: Change Leadership Emotional Intelligence – The People Side of Change

What is change leadership? Change leadership is really about leading the people who will be implementing the change; the employees you need to make the change happen and be sustainable. Most leaders are confused. They think that we should refer to change leadership as change management. Change management implies that leaders "manage" their employees. How silly. In order for real change to be effectively implemented, leaders need to use change leadership techniques and strategies that increase employee engagement, motivation, productivity, and the likelihood to get the change actually implemented. They just don't understand that people resist change because they are people. Furthermore, most leaders frequently don't know how to facilitate change in their organizations effectively. They lack the understanding and skills to employ Change Leadership Emotional Intelligence while leading change, and they don't employ effective change leadership strategies.

## Change Leadership Emotional Intelligence (CLEI)

Emotional Intelligence [3], as a psychological theory, was explored by Peter Salovey and John Mayer. Daniel Goleman [1] talked about the Emotional Intelligence framework having five competencies: self-awareness, self- management, motivation, social awareness, and social skills. CLEI combines similar fundamental competency underpinnings with critical specifics to leading change. These competencies of change leadership are not stages, and are not necessarily sequential. The effective leader uses these competencies throughout the change leadership process. CLEI helps inform the leader in making decisions regarding change leadership strategies.

So, what are the competencies and just what do they mean? The supporting competencies of CLEI are Change Self-Awareness, Change Self-Management, Change Motivation, Change Social Awareness, and Change Social Skills. Not only do you have to be intelligent in a traditional sense to implement change, but also you have to have CLEI to effectively onboard and motivate your employees to change. Just because leaders are smart, and have good management skills, it doesn't mean they know how nor have the ability to lead change with an understanding of emotional intelligence.

The first competency leg, Change Self-Awareness, involves leaders needing to continually evaluate their own change leadership skills and deficits, such as how to coach and communicate in change, and how to implement best practices. It means that they need to be aware of their own emotional feelings about the change. Is the leader feeling frustrated, anxious and resentful about the change? Does the leader have the self-confidence to lead during change?

The second leg, Change Self-Management, involves the leaders self-managing their thoughts and feelings about change, about how it is being implemented, and about the anticipated outcomes. Do the leaders maintain a level of composure and positivity about the change or do the leaders, consumed with fear, openly share worries, resentment and anger about the change to their employees? Do the leaders vent with employees as a way to convince the employees that the change wasn't their idea, or to convince the employees of their own skepticism as to whether the change will actually be implemented effectively? How leaders express themselves will affect every employee with whom they interact with. Do the employees trust their leaders? Are the leaders conscientious about the team's performance? Are the leaders flexible and innovative, and willing to hear ideas from others to ensure successful implementation of the change?

Change Motivation, the third competency of this framework, deals with the leaders' commitment to achieve excellence. Do the leaders align themselves with the goals of the organization? Do the leaders have initiative, and are the leaders optimistic? All of these questions are important to support and motivate themselves and others during change.

The fourth competency of CLEI, Change Social Awareness, is where the leader empathizes and understands what his or her employees are feeling as part of the change. Does the leader coach the employees, listening to the pain, feelings and losses that the employees might experience as part of the change? Or, does the leader ignore the employees and use primarily command-and-control leadership? Does the leader only empathize with the follower, but does the leader empathize with the organization and the organizational leaders to whom he or she reports? Does the leader work to develop the skills of employees, leveraging diversity and reading the team's emotional states?

Change Social Skills, the fifth competency leg of CLEI, involves the leader's ability to effectively move the employee or employees to progress positively to implement and sustain the change? How does the leader communicate? How often? When? And, can the leader effectively coach employees to be engaged, actually embracing the change? Has the leader written a change leadership plan that engages employees? Does the leader coach in a manner where employees discover their roles and are engaged in their own problem-solving? Even if the leader has a handle on the first four competencies, he (or she) will not succeed in leading the change if deficient with the final leg: Change Social Skills.

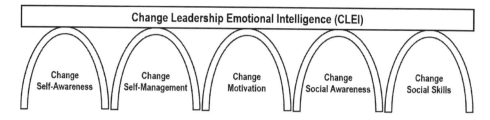

## *Change Self-Awareness*

Emotional self-awareness; accurate self-assessment (How are you doing emotionally with the organizational changes? How are you dealing with the ambiguity? Are you mad, sad or depressed?)

## *Change Self-Management*

Self-control about your feelings (How are you managing your emotions and loss? Do you feel like you are sharing too many negative feelings with your employees? How are you taking care of yourself? Are you ready to coach?)

## *Change Motivation*

Motivating self and others (Are you motivated to lead implementation of the organizational change? Can you motivate your employees?)

## *Change Social Awareness*

Empathy (Do you know how your employees feel and what they think they might lose as part of the change?)

## *Change Social Skills*

Moving your employees in a positive direction (Are you intentionally choosing the best change strategies and providing change coaching?)

This competency framework will be further outlined in Section 2 describing each leg.

# Chapter 3: Common CLEI Mistakes

Approximately 50% - 90% of all change events result in failure. Although organizations use successful tools such as Lean and other change techniques, they're very frequently disappointed in the results or outcomes. Corporations, businesses and other organizations understand the necessity of change but they often need assistance in implementing it effectively. Leaders are often so consumed with what needs to be changed – the timelines, the overall project plan, and how to manage it – that they forget about the people who will ultimately carry out the plan and will be most affected by it.

Simply put, most companies and organizations do not know how to lead people, nor do they know how to develop effective change management plans that use effective strategies. While company leaders may be excellent project managers, they do not understand the importance and the elements of an effective change leadership. The following scenarios will likely resonate with most leaders. These scenarios illustrate the change mistakes that leaders often make when not using CLEI or other effective change leadership strategies.

## Mistake #1 – Forgetting the People: Who Are All Those People?

Leaders know they need to implement changes. Often, they know it is the best thing for the organization, but sometimes they get confused. They think that developing a project management plan is all they need to do. They believe if they figure out what needs to be done, and when it needs to be done, that everyone will jump merrily on the change wagon to implement the change that has been planned so well. However, many times leaders forget about the people. They simply do not know that people have the power to stop change or implement change. This oversight can cost leaders. The change event will probably result in failure. All the planning and all the resources count for nothing because the leaders forgot the people. They didn't consider the employees, employee engagement, or even give credit for making changes. Ignoring the people will result in lowered morale, lower employee engagement and productivity, and may even result in sabotage.

*Kevin was passionate about launching the IT solution enterprise-wide. It was innovative, cutting edge, and useful. He knew that the users in the company would love using the system. He carefully and deliberately identified the necessary steps, resources, timelines and people responsible for initiation, planning, execution, construction, monitoring, and completion dates. He checked out each resource to ensure that it would indeed be available when the new solution was launched. He developed charts and tables electronically to identify milestones and outcomes. He printed the charts and displayed them where everyone could see them. When it came time to launch the new product, many employees expressed their disbelief and anger with a new system. Kevin could not understand why the employees were not more excited. He was frustrated when milestones were not met. He adjusted his project management plan and revised dates for completion. Although each task and activity seemed to be relatively easy, employees seemed to fight each and every step. Kevin couldn't understand why the employees would resist such a great new solution that was easy to use and would benefit each employee immensely.*

In this scenario, Kevin lacked the fourth leg of CLEI (Change Social Awareness) and fifth leg (Change Social Skills). He lacked understanding of how his employees felt about the change and what the employees might anticipate that they were losing during this IT implementation. He didn't coach people, nor did he have a change leadership plan that complemented the project management plan.

Let there be no mistake; for any significant organizational change, it is critical to have a project management plan. However, it is equally important to have a change leadership plan that involves many employees and spells out the important people-changing events that need to happen: training, inclusion, decision making, celebrations, constant communication, and effective leadership coaching for employees. Without the change leadership plan, the project plan is ineffective. Without leaders who coach their employees, the change will probably end in failure, regardless how well thought out the project management plan was developed.

## Mistake #2 – Micromanaging the Followers: Telling Them What to Do

Sometimes leaders believe they are in their positions so they can direct (or over-direct) employees to do things the way the leader wants. It is surprising that even the most brilliant leaders actually believe that micromanagement is an effective way to lead. They are always surprised and bitter that employees don't listen or follow this leadership, and employees are disengaged. In actuality, a command-and-control model should only be used in crisis situations, whether the situation requires change or not.

Often leaders band together with other high-level leaders and formulate a plan for change execution. After much discourse, they arrive at a plan of execution. They work hard on their plan and carefully consider it, outlining every detail of the change implementation. After the development of this plan, they make a grand announcement to staff to tell them what is going to happen. They don't spend a lot of time discussing the change with employees, they just tell them what to do and how they are to do it. During the course of the implementation, the leaders provide feedback to their teams, telling them to work faster and more efficiently or telling them how the change implementation will deviate from the original plan. They are masters at micromanaging. The leaders analyze problems and identify solutions. The employees are expected to do what they are told. But, the problem is that it just doesn't work. It doesn't work because peoples' brains are wired for autonomy. David Rock [4]talks about how micromanagement can generate a threat response in peoples' minds. When this happens, uncertainty is aroused and stress levels are increased such that humans cannot think creatively, can't work well with others, and can't make informed decisions. When employees are micromanaged, their brains feel the threat.

*John held a business degree and worked his way up in several manufacturing companies. He was a Lean expert, having accumulated years of continuous quality improvement experiences and being black belt certified. He was confident, bright, ambitious and hardworking. As the operations manager, he was committed to having a heightened return on investment regarding the manufacturing of a newly competitive product. He knew exactly how to manufacture the product and develop the most effective schedule. The schedule would require changing the operations from one shift to a daytime and a swing shift. The level of detail he put into the change execution was extraordinary. He identified which staff members would work during each shift, and developed manufacturing processes for both. It was a perfect plan. He announced his plan to the supervisors and staff. He shared the elaborate plans and told the supervisors how they would implement the processes. During the management team meeting, supervisors pushed back and identified many reasons the plan wouldn't work. John couldn't understand it. Why weren't they onboard? The objections were thinly veiled excuses and lacked any sound thinking. Perhaps the supervisors and staff were just stupid? John told them to implement the plan and processes or they could expect a possible reassignment. In frustration, John attended several all-hands meetings where he detailed his expectations.*

*Employees sat silently listening while looking at their phones. Following the meeting, John heard that morale had plummeted further, and several of the key employees were looking for other work. Manufacturing targets were missed and the product line was in jeopardy. John could not understand how this happened.*

In this scenario, John understood his own feelings, and shared his excitement and motivation, but lacked the fourth leg of CLEI (Change Social Awareness) and the fifth leg (Change Social Skills). He lacked understanding of how his employees felt about the change, and what they might anticipate losing during this new process implementation. He didn't coach his supervisors, nor did he have a change leadership plan that complemented the project management plan. If he had had a change leadership plan, it would have included a better communication strategy, change-training, coaching activities, and employee involvement and recognition activities.

Using command-and-control during change is usually inappropriate and ineffective. The exception to this rule is during a crisis. When fighting a fire, the leader doesn't try to involve staff in an exit strategy and doesn't promote inclusion. The leader directs employees in an exit plan that lets employees get out safely. If an organization has a real and urgent threat that requires a change to be implemented quickly, it is effective for a leader to use a command type leadership to implement the change. However, the command-and-control style is used much too often for many change events, resulting in the leaders actually sabotaging the change event by not including others in the planning and decision-making, and denying them autonomy in executing the plan. Telling people when and how to do tasks usually results in push backs, lowered productivity, and general resistance to the change from all levels.

# Mistake #3 – Forgetting to Do the Homework: Making Decisions Based on Hunches

Many leaders implement change without asking some very relevant questions before the change is actually planned for and implemented. Do our supervisors know how to be effective coaches and leaders? Are they trained to be leaders? Are the employees engaged? Are the work teams intact, or rather dysfunctional and sick? Poor leaders make the mistake of believing that their teams are adequate, or they decide that they don't have time to perform some diagnostics. Spending some time asking, answering, and addressing these questions will lead to a more successful change implementation. Moving ahead without having a discussion, diagnostics, or a thought process inventory will lead to bigger and greater problems later that will compromise the success of the change event.

*Maureen was excited to be given the new responsibility of leading the customer service unit. This unit would be working with some new customer accounts from out of the country. There were three large teams within the customer service unit, with supervisors assigned to each team. Maureen was aware that one team was particularly toxic but was unsure of the other groups. She believed that they were well managed, but she wasn't sure. Certainly, this new venture of adding out-of-country customers would energize the employees and supervisors who often presented themselves as lacking initiative, motivation and were generally disengaged. Maureen was certain she could motivate them with this exciting change. But when Maureen and the supervisory team launched the change, she was surprised with the lack of leadership and coaching skills exhibited by the supervisors. One of the leaders was totally disengaged, and one of the leaders was committed to the change but was a micromanager. The remaining supervisor thought the change was all wrong, and shared his feelings with his followers. The change implementation wasn't working.*

*Customer service agents were calling in sick frequently, customers were complaining, the call waiting times were unacceptable, and Maureen was being asked by her leadership why they should keep her.*

In this scenario Maureen lacked the fourth leg of CLEI (Change Social Awareness) and fifth leg of CLEI (Change Social Skills). She lacked any understanding of how her employees or supervisors felt about the change. She didn't understand the supervisors' general leadership styles or their change leadership skills. They weren't trained to lead, nor were they trained specifically how to lead during change. She didn't evaluate the employees' level of engagement nor did she address the toxic teams prior to the change.

Diagnosing potential issues that might jeopardize the implementation of the change, prior to the change event itself, can take place in a variety of ways. The leader might sit down with some subordinates and ask some questions, or meet with teams during staff meetings or focus groups. The leader might consider administering some quick assessments to employees. Using assessments is a phenomenal way to gather data and use the data to make a plan to address issues. If the leader discovers the team is dysfunctional or has poor morale, the leader might suggest some team-building activities. If the supervisors or directors lack important leadership and coaching skills, a consultant may be brought in or the leaders might attend some workshops to develop skills. The assessments can be used over and over again to see if there are changes or new areas of concern. The assessments serve as a baseline.

## Mistake #4 – Playing the Blame Game: Better to Blame Others than take Responsibility

More often than not, leaders are angry about the change. They might be worried about what they will lose and how much work it might entail, or they might wonder why the change is being considered in the first place. We all like predictability to some extent. We know our work; we know how to do it, so why does it need to change? What will it mean for us as leaders? Will we be blamed if it doesn't work? Will the organization discontinue or the company be bought out? Leaders have the exact same fears and concerns that their employees experience. Being a leader doesn't make you exempt from natural human reactions.

It is normal to feel anger and anxiety about change and to grieve the loss of what will be left behind. Instead of reflecting upon their own personal fears and anticipated losses associated with the change, leaders often blame others as being the reason for the necessity of the change. Often leaders express their anger to their employees, blaming human resources, upper management or others for the pending change. By blaming others, they create a dysfunctional and unproductive workforce that resists the change.

*Angelo was really unhappy with the direction the organization was going. The CEO and Board of Trustees wanted to decentralize staff and offices to better meet the needs of clients. The nonprofit served homeless people within the city. There was a change being made to open smaller offices throughout the city as well as several in outlying areas. "How ridiculous," thought Angelo. What would the organization do with their current lease? Who would find new spaces? How could they afford the rent? If services decentralized, would that mean the organization doesn't need him? What would happen to him? Would he be demoted like the leaders that were laid off in the 1990's downsizing fad? During the team meeting, Angelo expressed his anger toward management's decision, citing reasons why it would never work. Angelo later learned that renting the other office spaces was very doable and that the leaders planned to give him a raise for the additional responsibilities. Although Angelo's attitude had changed, he found his staff to be angry, disgruntled and resistive of the change.*

In this scenario, Angelo lacked four legs of CLEI: the second leg (Change Self-Control),the third leg (Change Motivation), the fourth leg (Change Social Awareness), and the fifth leg (Change Social Skills). He lacked any understanding of how sharing his feelings about the change would affect his followers. He lacked motivation and initiative. He didn't have empathy or trust in his organization or the organizational leaders. He didn't know how his employees felt; nor could he help them implement the change since he had already sabotaged the change event by spewing his emotional vomit on his employees.

Although Angelo certainly had normal emotional responses to the change, he shouldn't have used his employees as his sounding board. By using his team to express his concerns, he contaminated them with his negative emotion and created more resistance to the pending change.

# Mistake #5 – Not Coaching Employees: Believing Employees Will Hear It and Just Do It

During change implementation, many managers are overworked, overwhelmed and short of time. Their constant efforts are geared toward milestones, productivity goals and service outcomes. Most leaders, during change, hope their employees will understand the importance of the change and get on-board with their roles and do their work independently. Most managers don't have coaching skills, and even when they do, they don't know how to coach during change. Oddly, during change employees need their supervisors' coaching and support more than ever. They need help in figuring out what the change means, how it impacts them, what role they have; and the reassurance and support that they will be able to perform their jobs successfully.

*Bill was responsible for the acquisition of a company. There was so much to do. Bill shared the vision of the acquisition, as well as the new expectations required of existing and new employees. He had an excellent communication plan and even engaged employees from all levels in planning for the acquisition activities. Yet, supervisors and employees seemed to be floundering. They expressed resistance to the change. The new employees told Bill they didn't feel welcome and the other employees expressed their concern with the employees who were on-boarded as part of the acquisition. Employees and supervisors were unclear about what roles they were to perform. Bill knew employees needed to get on-boarded so that the acquisition could successfully be implemented. Bill re-sent an earlier email that had been sent out the month before outlining the new vision, strategy and roles. Despite his efforts, employees were calling in sick, were not performing, and were spending a lot of time complaining to each other. No productivity goals were being met.*

In this scenario, Bill primarily lacked the fourth leg of CLEI (Change Social Skills). Although Bill included staff and communicated well, he was unaware of the importance of coaching his supervisors, as well as the importance of supervisors coaching their employees. Bill and his supervisors lacked the knowledge and skill levels that were required to lead employees during this change.

During change, leaders need to spend more time with employees rather than less time. It is somewhat counterintuitive. Leaders are busier during the change and they need to be focused on the details of the change at hand. Leaders need to spend more time with employees, providing them with encouragement, coaching and support. Any coaching effort must entail an understanding of the perceived and real losses employees might experience, and must use a coaching strategy specifically tailored to supporting followers during change.

# Mistake #6 – Neglecting Change Training: Thinking Change Skills are Intuitive

Change leadership is different than project management. A leader's skill set during change is sometimes counterintuitive and requires many additional skills already possessed by more seasoned leaders. Leaders often dismiss the need for *change leadership* and *follower change training.*

*Bethany knew how she could make work happen. She was a great project manager and knew exactly how to organize things to get work done. She was considered to be an adequate or even a good leader. But when the medical clinic care delivery model was transforming to a trauma informed care approach, she was at a loss. Employees did not understand the culture change. They were resisting the change and were not following through on activities. She wasn't certain how to lead them. The employees seemed to be resisting the change just because the approach was different. The employees didn't present any rationale reasons why the change wouldn't work.*

Typically, leaders wrongly believe that implementing change is not something they need to learn. They believe it is intuitive and more aligned with a command-and-control approach. Sadly, it is only after a change event failure that they contemplate what went wrong. The odds that a change event is successfully implemented are enhanced when leaders – meaning supervisors, operation managers, directors, CEOs, and board members – attend training to learn basic skills and learn why these skills are important.

In addition to leaders participating in change training, it is equally important for employees without leadership responsibilities to participate in training as well. If employees know how change affects them as well as others, more employees will be inclined to be engaged and support their colleagues. They will be less likely to resist the changes and more likely to engage in behaviors needed for the change (e.g. positive attitude, increased productivity, commitment to stay at the company or organization).

With this mistake of underestimating the need for change training, leaders primarily miss out on the fourth and fifth legs of CLEI (Change Social Awareness and Change Social Skills respectively). These leaders don't evaluate the other leaders' or followers' emotions and skills and don't utilize training to develop their employees.

Training is more likely to stick for employees/leaders if neuroscience principles are followed. Davachi, Kiefer, Rock and Rock [5], talked about the AGES learning model, which includes increasing participants' *Attention* to learning (minimizing distractions and making sure learner is focusing). Make sure there are no distractions during the training. *Generation-* where the learner is motivated to understand and apply knowledge in their own way. Enable leaders/employees to apply learning to their own change events that have occurred or are occurring. Use training opportunities that incorporate more application than lecture. *Emotions-* Using emotions to help people learn and make training positive. Provide a positive emotional learning experience where employees can connect with others and receive feedback. Encourage staff to learn about change management, and support them when they return to the workplace. *Spacing-* whenever possible, provide short segments of training over a period of time.

# Mistake #7 – Ousting the Employees: Leaving Them Out Again

As mentioned previously, leaders often like to command and control the change way too often. They feel confident and empowered to make decisions and direct most aspects of change. They frequently omit

Employees are angry and frustrated, and they push back on the change. Yet, leaders continually attempt to use this ridiculous approach.

*Mark was leading a group of engineers to design a medical device that was a very exciting and innovative product. Although the company had many established and profitable products already developed, Mark knew that upper leadership wanted his team to explore new options. Mark thought it would be a good idea to tell his employees that if they didn't develop a new competitive product, they might be without a job. When he announced the details and the threat, Mark was surprised that his employees were not excited about the product. In fact, his top engineers were looking for other work with a competitor. Mark couldn't understand why the engineers weren't excited about the new product.*

*Miguel's group had recently implemented a new design system that portrayed products in 3-D. The group hadn't had a lot of training but had implemented the new system anyway. Most of the team members were slow at producing their product. Miguel thought it was time to motivate his employees. He told them that if they didn't meet the deadline, he would recommend that those employees not receive a company-wide salary increase. To his surprise, his team didn't meet targets the following month; in fact, they were further behind than previous months.*

In these situations, the leaders lacked the fourth and the fifth legs of CLEI (Change Social Awareness and Change Social Skills respectively). The leaders didn't have empathy for the followers, considering how the employees would feel (Change Social Awareness), nor did the leaders know that threatening employees won't motivate them (Change Social Awareness). In both of these situations, employees were clearly not motivated by threats or urgency. In fact, they behaved in counterproductive ways, actually jeopardizing the organization's sustainability. The threat or urgency was heard by employees, and their response was a lack of productivity and their intention to leave the company.

Leaders need to know how to motivate employees during change. Motivating employees doesn't mean threatening employees. Motivating employees or engaging employees happens through including staff in information and decision making. It is making employees feel like a vital part of the company where they know their role. It is not to say that if there is real urgency, that leaders don't discuss it, but it cannot be the sole means to motivate employees. Those leaders who foolishly attempt to play the urgency card will be bitterly disappointed.

## Mistake #11 – Playing Hush-Hush: Being Silent

Most leaders play the hush-hush game during change. Researchers and writers refer to this phenomenon as "organizational silence" [6] [7] [8]. I have found that leaders resist communicating honestly and openly to their staff. They either don't trust them with information, don't think they can handle it, or they want to wait until the change is totally understood and can be articulated. This mistake often breaks the trust between management and employees. This trust is commonly referred to as a psychological contract between the company and the leader. Once that trust is broken, research shows that it is hard to build back.

When employees don't hear information and updates, they often engage in negative talk, speculating what might happen, and consequently emotionally vomiting on each other. Employees don't stand around the water cooler discussing how management is brilliant and that they know that they will be taken care of. Don't trick yourself with this belief. Instead, they talk with each other, fabricating worst-case scenarios that only bring morale down and decrease employee engagement.

*Everyone at the plastics manufacturing company knew that their company was probably going to be bought by another company. Certainly management was aware of the acquisition developments but thought it would be better to wait until the details were clearly developed before they shared how the acquisition would play out. As a daily ritual, the employees would gather in clusters imagining what would happen. Employees were less interested in their work and more interested in talking about how the change would unfold. Productivity tanked. Leaders knew they would need to share information but still thought that this wasn't the right time.*

Waiting to provide information is a mistake. Employees' brains are better primed for change when they get information and updates. I often encourage leaders to share the current change vision or change plans whenever they have updates. I suggest that leaders add "this might change" when they describe change visions and plans. If leaders wait until the change is entirely known, it is usually too late and employees have already written their story of change.

Providing information through every modality, including email, discussions, all-hands meetings, written notes, is important; employees have more trust in leaders who are willing to be honest and authentic, who trust them with information and care about them. Silent leaders during change are usually regarded as incompetent or untrustworthy and suspect.

Don't play the hush-hush game. Talk. Tell people what you know. Tell them the information you have now, but tell them it might change.

# Mistake #12 – Neglecting the Plan: Planning Without the Employees in Mind

Leaders are more often interested in project management plans than leadership plans. Those leaders who write only a project plan are asking for failure. Certainly, they will have the giant charts, timelines, milestones and people responsible, yet the project management doesn't serve to motivate people to do their work. No one is coaching the followers. No one is coaching their supervisors. These leaders focus only on outcomes, falsely believing that stating goals and activities will serve as a motivational tool for everyone.

*Miguel led a team in Costa Rica. He was responsible for a new microwave product that would be used on defense planes. The product change was significant and so was the process, but the work needed to be done in two months. He didn't have much time to get his team properly organized and the team needed to get on board with the project quickly. His team helped him write a project management plan but there wasn't enough time for the change leadership plan, nor was it thought there was a need to do one. Thirty days into the project, the team was behind deadline. Morale had plummeted. Miguel thought that maybe the project plan wasn't comprehensive enough, but he couldn't think of what he could have added to the plan. He couldn't think of a thing he had missed.*

Miguel lacked the fourth leg of CLEI (Change Social Skills). He didn't know how he could move followers forward during change. He didn't acknowledge what needed to happen nor could he implement the skills and strategies necessary to move them forward. Leaders need to write change management plans even when the turnaround is quick. Without that plan, leaders forget to communicate to the employees in a robust manner. They usually don't include staff, don't motivate them and then wonder why another change that they implemented didn't work.

# Mistake #13 – Dismissing the Past with Bitter Goodbyes: Painting the "Old Ways" as Horrific

*Jeff wanted his staff to understand that the new processing standard was better than what the organization had been using for decades. Although his staff had done the previous process well, upper management wanted Jeff and his team to try a new approach. Jeff wanted everyone to get on board quickly, so he held an all-hands meeting. He told them that the new process was improved and that it would be much better than what the team had produced in the past. He proceeded to tell them that the old process was antiquated, ineffective and a waste of resources. He followed his discussion with a description of how great the new process would be. Instead of his employees seeming interested in embracing the new process, the employees seemed angry and resistant.*

Jeff lacked the fourth and fifth legs of CLEI. He didn't have empathy to understand how his employees felt pride in the work they did before (Change Social-Awareness) and he didn't know that by dismissing the "old", that employees would feel disengaged from trying anything new (Change Social Skills). It is important to say our goodbyes to the old process, standards, products, etc.. Saying goodbye helps people move on to the new. Bridges told us that we need to talk about the endings and we need to create actions that show that something is ending. But it is important that the leader does not negate the past in hopes of creating passion for the change. Bridges reminded us to treat the past with respect, and the past should never be denigrated [9]. By dismissing the past and the work that was done, employees usually feel that the leader does not value them and they become demoralized. The leader needs to help employees let go of the past but must do it in a way where employees feel valued and good about their work. The leader needs to create an excitement about the new change without discounting the work previously performed. Instead of saying, "What you did was not as efficient as it could have been," the leader might say, "I have confidence in all of you. The work you did in the past was well done, and, with all of you doing this new process, I know that we will even be better." See the difference?

# Mistake #14 – Forgetting the Party: Failing to Recognize or Celebrate

Sometimes leaders are so busy leading a change event, monitoring the progressing, and setting new goals, that they neglect the celebrations. Once a goal is met, there is a new goal, and the leader is concentrating on the new milestone.

*William was feeling the pressure. He had to increase sales by 10%. Last month, his team was required to increase sales by 10%. The group exceeded the goal by 12%, but now his leadership was asking for an additional 10%. William worked with his group to put together a plan to increase sales with a quick turnover. Everyone was exhausted, barely meeting the goal that week. William didn't know how the team could go on. He developed an aggressive and tiring plan that his sales account managers would increase the number of cold calls they would make. When he presented his detailed plan, many team members said they felt like there was little recognition for the work done and didn't want to increase sales. William couldn't understand their negativity. They needed to work harder not less.*

William lacked leg five of CLEI (Change Social Skills). Employees need to celebrate accomplishments and be recognized for their hard work. Even if the celebration is a quick lunch or deliberate team recognition, the accolades are valued by employees and serve as a motivation to reach new goals. William didn't understand that recognition was a strategy to increase productivity and morale.

# Mistake #15 – Ignoring Self-Care: A Fast Trip to Burn Out

Change is tough. Change is pain for everyone. According to neuroscientists, when people hear of change, they feel pain. A leader who is effective at leading should be exhausted, because it is exhausting to lead change effectively. Leading change without considering change management principles is less arduous than leading change with the people in mind. For leaders who want to lead a successful change management event, they must be taking care of themselves. Whether this is via exercise, meditation, eating right or sleeping well, leaders needs to take care of themselves first.

*Kelly was a company executive. She was smart, capable and a great leader. She used CLEI and used many change strategies effectively. Her staff was happy and was moving positivity with the change implementation. Kelly was working night and day and working every weekend. She stopped exercising and barely had time to eat properly. She didn't sleep well. She was exhausted and stressed. Her family missed seeing her and complained regularly. Although Kelly was successful at leading the change well, she was considering finding new leadership employment. She needed to find a job that wasn't as stressful.*

Think about the safety demonstrations on an airplane before taking off. The flight attendant instructs us that in the case of an emergency, the oxygen devices will drop from the ceiling. We are instructed to put our oxygen apparatuses on first before helping others. The same is true for a change event. We have to make sure we are doing well if we are going to lead others effectively. Leading change is hard work, and we need to take care of ourselves. What are you doing to take care of yourself? Are you exercising? Sleeping? Eating right? Enjoying time off?

## Mistake #16 – Dismissing Employees' Emotional Responses: Didn't Think About Losses

One of the biggest mistakes leaders can make is ignoring the emotional responses of employees, seeing them as a hindrance to employees actually embracing change. They mistakenly believe that suppressing emotions will lead to success. They tell their followers to get over their emotions. The leaders do their very best to ignore emotions in hopes that employees will feel good about the change. They don't use the emotional responses of employees to guide managerial actions and provide interventions that will actually increase the likelihood of a quicker return on the investment. They don't consider what the employee might be "losing" as part of the change.

*Andrea was hearing her employees' concerns about the change. People were anxious and getting frustrated. The team members started to blame each other for work not being completed, and the morale was low. Every time Andrea picked up on even a hint of depressing conversation, she cut the discussion off, telling everyone that they needed to get down to business and not waste time with feelings. Her team stopped talking about the change and their feelings. Now three of the employees call in sick frequently and two others were found to be looking for other work during time they were supposed to be working.*

Poor Andrea. She didn't understand the importance of people's feelings (lack of Change Social Awareness), nor did she know what to do if people were expressing sad feelings and emotions (lack of Change Social Skills). Andrea and many leaders miss the opportunity to think about the emotions employees are experiencing and to use those feelings to devise a strategy to improve morale, in turn, they fail to develop the coaching skills to help people through the work transition. Kiefer [10] indicated that leaders need to consider the emotional landscape of organizations during changes. She said instead of seeing emotions as irrational and dysfunctional, leaders should see emotions as a vital part of change and should differentiate managerial actions based on emotions.

Even when leaders recognize that their employees are struggling with a change, many do not have the coaching skills to help the employees. This can result in decreased productivity and in some cases, employees leaving the company and seeking employment elsewhere. Asking employees to talk about how they are doing and listening to feelings helps the managers identify potential strategies, such as a fun and productive team-building activity. Finding out what the employees may perceive as what they are "losing" as a result of the change helps detangle some of the change resistance. Then, the employees can begin to find hope and opportunity in the change.

All of these common mistakes that leaders make add up and result in change failure, not because leaders didn't develop a comprehensive project management plan, but because they didn't know how they felt emotionally, they didn't manage their own feelings, they weren't self-motivated, they didn't have empathy for their leaders and followers, and they just couldn't move people forward.

Before discussing the complexities of CLEI, we need to talk about what every employee, regardless of his or her level in the organization, might feel about the anticipated change. The next chapter will be talking about some of the losses that people anticipate or experience during change, and why all employees are critical for productivity and sustainability. If a leader doesn't acknowledge the losses an individual might perceive, it is unlikely that the leader will be able to help the employee see the hope and opportunities related to the change.

When employees don't feel security, they may reduce their productivity and, even worse, the employees may want to leave the organization. Often the best employees find work with another organization more quickly than the poorly performing employees. By making employees feel insecure, leaders are left with a marginalized workforce doing marginal work.

Often this occurs because management has gone hush-hush. During change, most leaders believe that the change should be communicated once or twice but employee involvement in the change process is best avoided. Employees' feelings, questions and involvement are just too much work for leaders. Employees are expected to hear the change message and implement the change without any feelings, resistance or questions.

Only when it is true, leaders need to communicate that no further downsizing or layoffs are expected. Of course there are no guarantees in any organization or company, but reassuring employees that no further layoffs are expected assures the employees, and they feel more secure. When additional layoffs are anticipated, the leader must be authentic and honest.

## What LEADERS need to do

- Coach employees through negative thinking and help problem-solve and reassure them that their position and the organization is secure (only state this if it is true).
- Value the employee through praising and affirmations.
- Regularly acknowledge that the employee's work brings value to the company and is important, no matter what level of work they perform.
- Promote activities that increase inclusion.
- Ensure that communication is happening on all levels.

- Celebrate successes of change.

# Competence

Sometimes people feel like they no longer have the skills necessary to do the job or feel like they can't learn new job skills to perform newly assigned work, perhaps due to reorganization, a new product, or assignment to new tasks. Employees feel a competency loss that actually plays out as paralyzing. Incompetency feelings lead to an inability to learn or actively produce.

Leaders often mistakenly believe their employees can learn any new task. Often employees can, but they may need reassurance and may need additional training and check-ins. Employees will rarely approach the leader and admit that they need help or training or talk about their worries.

## *What LEADERS need to do*

- Coach employees to help identify needed skills or behaviors.
- Promote development activities and affirm that everyone can benefit from ongoing development.
- Support employees in identifying training strategies.
- Allow employees to make mistakes in learning.
- Celebrate successes and accomplishments.

# Control

Many employees express feeling a loss of control during change. They may experience a loss of autonomy and may feel threatened by their bosses micromanaging or threatening them to comply. Employees report that others are making decisions on their behalf. Where before they had the control to do their work and make decisions regarding their work processes, they report being micromanaged and directed to do things without their involvement or input. Employees report that their bosses make threatening statements during change such as "get onboard or else!" Leaders making all the decisions for employees, and/or threatening them, just doesn't work with their brains. Rock and Schwartz [11]reported that threats are manually taxing to the employee, and they result in responses that may reduce the employee's productivity. We don't like threats, and we will push against them. Employees will resist micromanagement, whether by leaving an organization, decreasing our productivity, or even sabotaging the work.

During change, leaders wrongly assume that they are responsible for creating every solution for every problem and "fixing" everything. By fixing everything, solving every problem, and micromanaging every step of the employees' work, the employee actually resists the change— even if it is the most remarkable change ever created. Employees will fight the change.

## What LEADERS need to do

- Allow employees to take risks and make mistakes.
- Don't micromanage.
- Whenever possible, allow for employees to make decisions about their work processes or other work related issues.
- If there is a new work process, assure employees that they will master the work and will be working independently soon.
- Coach employees through negative thinking, and help problem-solve and reassure.
- Promote activities that increase inclusion.
- Ensure that communication is happening on all levels.
- Celebrate successes.

# Identity

If employees have had a change in the work they perform or think they will perform, they may have less of an identity. This occurs when perhaps their body of work has changed or, more likely, a change in job title to a lesser status. They experience loss of pride in their work, embarrassed by their new tasks. Perhaps because of a downsizing or reorganization, they are being asked to do lesser work. They no longer are proud of their work or their role, and they believe they are no longer valued at the work place.

Leaders usually change organizational structure because of diminishing resources, restructuring, mergers or downsizing. Leaders sometimes make these critical decisions to actually help retain jobs. What they don't understand is that as a result of these dramatic changes, the morale of the teams usually becomes dramatically lower. Leaders are perplexed and frustrated with why the morale is so low when they believe employees should be grateful to have a job and continue working. Although it makes sense that employees should be grateful, it is actually a critical mistake to expect gratitude from employees. What employees need during this time is not a leader telling them they should be happy they have a job, but a leader who is supportive and understanding. If leaders want employees to be highly productive, they need to support staff during employees' losses. Leaders who get locked into believing employees should be grateful become angry and become ineffective leaders quickly.

## What LEADERS need to do

- Show and tell employees regularly they are value-added to the organization.
- Engage and value employees.

- Ensure that communication is happening on all levels.
- Celebrate successes.
- Acknowledge that previous work done, prior to the change, was well done.

# Territory

Sometimes when people are moved as part of the change – perhaps from one work space to another work space or to another building – they feel like their territory has been violated. Maybe they are working with a different group of people because of the change. Their regular routine of working in the same space is disrupted. Employees might seem upset or sad. Moving employees' locations can shake them up. Leaders often find employees are spending a lot of time talking about why the move was a poor decision made by management rather than working on their tasks.

Leaders are usually oblivious to the losses employees feel during a relocation, especially if the leader's location has remained the same. Leaders notice that the morale is lowered but are unsure why. Although this loss is significant, leaders can quickly increase morale. Before location changes are made, leaders can include employees in the move planning. Leaders can do easy team-building activities, such as bringing in pizza when employees are packing their items. The leader can organize some quick and fun activities or prizes. Then, even more importantly, when at the new space, a leader should suggest a potluck or team activity in the new space.

## What LEADERS need to do to

- Do not change employees' work spaces during other change unless absolutely necessary.

- If you do relocate employees, involve employees in decision-making regarding and/or planning the move.
- Promote activities that increase inclusion.
- Initiate team-building activities at the new sites.
- Ensure that communication is happening on all levels.
- Celebrate successes.

# Belonging

Leadership is critical when employees feel a loss of belonging. Neuroscience research has suggested that when people don't feel included, or when they feel excluded, they can actually see the kind of reaction in the brain that physical pain might cause [4]. First, the leader needs to be informed about how employees feel. Leaders need to know if employees feel like they are part of the team or displaced. Sometimes when people are working with new people, or not working with others that they have worked with in the past, they feel like they don't belong anymore. Perhaps their peers were laid off, their team was reconfigured, or the work place has been restructured and they have a new supervisor. Communication may be marginal and employees are engaging in rumor mills to determine their place or lack of place in the organization.

Leaders often like to wait until they know the whole change story before they communicate. After all, why should they upset their team with information that is inadequate? Too often, leaders wait until the change vision and resulting processes are clear and well defined before engaging employees in discussions. When this happens, employees are left to their own devices in developing narratives about how the organization is doomed; they don't belong and are no longer valued. In addition, whenever there are personnel changes, staff added to teams, lay-offs of teams, or new reporting structures, employees have lost that sense of security and belonging.

Leaders must be able to articulate the vision of the change as it evolves—not just when the vision has been finally defined to perfection. Leaders who engage in discussions with employees, sharing anticipated changes and allowing discussions with their employees, are more likely to address this loss area. Employees absolutely need to know they are valued and how they fit in the new vision or changes. Their role needs to be spelled out and discussed. Communication must happen often and frequently. Second, when employees' team membership reporting structures have changed, leaders have the responsibility to address the losses of feeling left out. By using team-building exercises, coaching opportunities and allowing employees to experience belonging within their new teams, leader's teams will increase productivity.

## What LEADERS need to do

- Greet and acknowledge each employee whenever possible. Do not walk by employees without acknowledging them. Even a simple greeting using their name is helpful.
- Coach employees, asking that they support their colleagues and include them in activities and decision-making.
- Engage and value employees. Tell them why they matter to the organization and to the team.
- Ensure all employees continually hear the change vision and understand their roles.
- Promote communication and team building activities that increase inclusion.
- Celebrate successes through team activities such as potlucks or team lunches.

# Trust

Frequently, many employees don't trust leadership in the organization. Then, when a change occurs, more employees don't trust leadership, and those who never trusted the organization become vocal and belligerent regarding leaderships intentions. It is important that the leadership maintain and build trust levels in the organization. Otherwise, instead of working, employees will often engage in counterproductive behavior-discussing conspiracy and other theories with their peers. Once trust is lost, it is hard to get it back.

How does leadership combat lack of trust? Leaders need to build trust through leadership behaviors such as genuinely caring about employees, being authentic and honest, coaching and providing increased communication that allows for difficult conversations.

Leaders need to genuinely care about employees and be able to show it. Caring means that they care about employees as people, as workers, and as an important part of the organizational structure. Some leaders care about some employees in certain roles but not others in different roles. Leaders sometimes dismiss lower level employees such as administrative support, shipping, and receiving personnel or custodians. A caring leader values every person regardless of their position. A caring leader cares about the employee, both personally and professionally; cares enough to ask how they are doing, how their weekend went, and how their job is going; smiles and greets each employee by name whenever possible. A caring leader asks how people feel and helps the employee see opportunities in challenging situations. Caring can build a supportive relationship, and so can be authentic.

Authentic leaders are honest. They tell people that change might change. They talk to their staff earlier rather than later about change and current thinking. They admit to staff when they are wrong, and own their mistakes. They admit to their own shortcomings. They are gracious with employees when the employees make mistakes. They are honest, authentic and transparent. They don't play games with employees but see them as a valued part of the organization. Whenever possible, they share as much information as they can with their employees, holding back little. Authentic leaders hold other leaders authentic, asking that their supervisors and managers be honest, transparent and hold true to promises.

Authentic leaders coach and have difficult conversations when necessary. They spend time with their leaders and ask what is important to the employee. They share observations of employees' poor behavior and performance in a caring but honest manner. They don't hold back on having difficult conversations with employees, but make sure the conversation is supportive and clear. Too often leaders observe bad behaviors and performance, and they tell everyone except the employee. This leadership behavior is inexcusable, ridiculous and shortsighted.

Being authentic means the leader is being caring, supportive, direct about poor performance and honest. Most leaders do not evoke trust from employees because they don't think they have to; they marginalize their employees or simply don't have the skills necessary to have difficult conversations with their employees.

## What LEADERS need to do to

- Greet and talk to employees.
- Show them you care by asking about their work.
- Be honest but not overly negative.
- Admit your mistakes.
- Trust employees and tell them information sooner rather than later.

- Engage in difficult conversations when it is necessary.

# Leadership Support

Research suggests that many people express dissatisfaction with their supervisor or leadership during change [13]. They notice that the leaders might not be engaging with them, and they might comment that the leaders are not supporting them. Their leaders are not engaging with them nor coaching them. Leaders are playing hush-hush and not communicating. Leaders are leaving them to their devices, letting them create their own narratives and perpetuate rumors. Employees don't feel valued, don't feel like they belong and don't feel secure.

Leaders are usually struggling themselves. They themselves are feeling losses and are worried. They are wondering if the organization might survive and are unclear of the direction and vision of the organization. Many feel that they do not have the time to spend communicating with and coaching employees. They believe that the focus should be on the work, productivity and deadlines. They believe that people's emotional responses need to be ignored, contained or dismissed. But by dismissing emotions and employees' emotional responses, they are missing the opportunity to evaluate what is happening in their group and the opportunity to implement leadership strategies.

It is imperative that leaders spend time with their employees during change, not check-out. They need to coach their employees so that their employees know how they fit in and are reminded of the change vision. Leaders need to ask employees about what they are thinking and feeling.

## *What LEADERS need to do*

- Participate in leadership training and change leadership training.

- Communicate the change vision often and engage employees in discussions.
- Ensure that communication is happening on all levels.
- Consider employees' emotions, to evaluate morale and implement leadership strategies.
- Coach employees to understand their losses and help them problem-solve and find hope and opportunities in situations.
- Promote activities that increase inclusion.
- Use caution to ensure that the leader doesn't poison with emotional vomit.
- Celebrate successes often.
- Acknowledge that work done prior to the change was well done.

Ignoring employees' emotional responses, specifically losses, is a leadership mistake. Expecting people to just "get over it and work" isn't realistic and will only result in lowered productivity and sabotage. Thinking employees will suddenly approach their leaders to tell them of their losses is not realistic. Leaders need to demonstrate good leadership by recognizing emotional loss happens during change, understanding their role in addressing losses, and having the knowledge and skill to implement effective leadership activities.

The next section, section two, is a deeper dive into CLEI. The reader will have the opportunity to take a CLEI assessment and learn more about what it means.

# Section 2: Change Leadership Emotional Intelligence (CLEI)

## Change Management Emotional Intelligence Pre-Test: How are you and your leaders doing?

Indicate your level of agreement using the scale 1—Strongly Disagree, 2—Disagree, 3—Agree, 4—Strongly Agree.

1. I am aware of my emotional feelings about a particular change.
2. Leaders from all levels are aware of their emotional feelings about a particular change.
3. I am able to contain my negative feelings and responses about the change when talking with others.
4. Leaders from all levels are able to contain their negative feelings and responses about the change when talking with others.
5. I am able to coach employees to see the hope and opportunity of change events.
6. Leaders from all levels are able to coach their employees to see the hope and opportunity of change events.
7. I am able to empathize with employees regarding their feelings and thoughts about change.
8. Leaders from all levels are able to empathize with employees regarding their feelings and thoughts about change.
9. I am able to help employees move forward in successful implementation of change.
10. Leaders from all levels are able to help employees move forward in successful implementation of change.

*Score:*

*Key:*

*38 or above – Exceptional*

*30 to 37 – Good with development opportunities*

*20 to 29 – Needs improvement*

*Below 20 – Need to address immediately*

So, what are the legs again and what do they mean? The underpinnings of change leadership emotional intelligence are Change Self-Awareness, Change Self-Management, Change Motivation, Change Social Awareness, and Change Social Skills.

The first leg, Change Self-Awareness, means leaders needs to continually evaluate their own change management skills and deficits, such as how to coach and communicate in change and implement best practices. It means that they need to be aware of their emotional feelings about the change. Is the leader frustrated, anxious, and resentful about the change?

The second leg, Change Self-Management, means leaders needs to manage their thoughts and feelings about change, yet still be authentic. The leader must remain flexible and nimble during the change. Also, the leader needs to be comfortable with the fluidity of the change, authentically hearing new ideas of how to implement the change whether the new ideas are coming from employees, colleagues or leaders.

Change Motivation, the third competency of this framework, deals with the leader's commitment to achieve and meet excellence. Does the leader align himself or herself with the goals of the organization? Does the leader have initiative, and is the leader optimistic? All these questions are important to support and motivate themselves and others during change.

The fourth leg of CLEI, Change Social Skills, is where the leader empathizes and understands what his or her employees are feeling as part of the change. Does the leader spend time hearing the employees talk about their pain, feelings and losses that might be experienced as part of the change? Or does the leader ignore the employees and use primarily command-and-control leadership?

Change Social Management, the final competency leg of CLEI, refers to the leader who can effectively help the employees to move positively forward to implement and sustain the change. How does the leader communicate? How often? When? Can the leader effectively coach employees, colleagues and other leaders to where they are actually engaged and are embracing the change? Has the leader written a change leadership plan that engages employees? Does the leader coach in a manner where employees are discovering their roles and are engaging in their own problem-solving? And, can they effectively manage change through collaboration and cooperation and creating team synergy?

# Chapter 5: Change Self-Awareness

The first competency leg, Change Self-Awareness, means that leaders need to continually evaluate their own change management skills and deficits, such as how to coach and communicate in change, and how to implement best practices. It means that they need to be aware of their emotional feelings about the change. Is the leader frustrated, anxious and resentful about the change? Does the leader have the confidence to lead during change?

Being self-aware means the leader needs to be honest about his or her skill levels and competencies. Does the leader even know what skills and change management knowledge is needed? Has the leader undergone a self-checklist of change leadership competencies and have those competencies been validated by employees? Change competencies include:

1. Being able to develop, write and communicate a clear change vision.
2. Engaging in meaningful change activities that include staff from all levels.
3. Being able to write a change management plan involving employees.
4. Coaching other leaders and employees to move forward in implementing the change.
5. Measuring and showing change progress.
6. Celebrating change accomplishments.
7. Rewarding employees.

Another key piece of self-awareness is the leader knowing how they feel about the change. What losses or gains might be in store for the leader? What is the leader emotionally feeling about the change? Is the leader angry? Frustrated? Irritated? Happy? Resentful? Knowing how one feels means that the leader needs to be reflective and have quiet time to identify and sit with his or her emotions. It is necessary for leaders to know how they are feeling because if they don't, they simply can't manage their feelings. Leaders who haven't undergone self-reflection, and are oblivious to their possible losses and feelings, will negatively impact their employees and their productivity.

Finally the leader needs to be confident about their change management skills. When the leader lacks confidence, employees quickly note the leader's insecurity and are unlikely to implement the change effort. Employees will question the change justification, the means to the end, and will probably intentionally or unintentionally sabotage the change vision and processes. The change leader needs to know their change skill levels, must know how they feel about the change, and must be confident in implementing change.

# Chapter 6: Change Self-Management

The second leg, Change Self-Management, means the leader needs to be managing their thoughts and feelings about change, yet still be authentic. The leader must remain flexible during the change. Also, the leader needs to be comfortable with the fluidity of the change, authentically hearing new ideas of how to implement the change—whether the new ideas are coming from employees, colleagues or leaders.

Does the leader maintain a level of composure and positivity about the change? Or does the leader openly share his or her worries, resentment and anger about the change to his or her employees? Does the leader vent with employees as a way to convince the employees it wasn't his or her idea, or convince the employees of his or her disbelief that the change will actually be implemented effectively? How leaders express themselves affects every employee they interact with.

Shawn Achor [18] talked about emotional contagion and how it works through our brains. He said that due to mirror neurons, specialized brain cells that parrot feelings, it is possible for emotions to spread from one person to another in a moment. What this means is that our emotions can infect a group of people in a heartbeat! Achor goes on to say that just like negative emotions, positive emotions are also contagious, which makes positive emotions a powerful tool. So, your emotions are critical to your group of employees, colleagues or others.

So how does a leader remain authentic and honest about the change while at the same time not spreading emotional vomit on the employees? The self-regulated leader knows how they feel. They have spent self-reflection time to identify the emotions they are feeling. They have worked through their anticipated losses, negative emotional responses and pain. But how can leaders do that? How can they genuinely identify their feelings and then turn around and be optimistic and encouraging to staff? Is it possible? It is possible, but it involves work.

Consider this situation: Robert had been leading his group to process the licensing requirements for nearly a decade. A Lean and continuous improvement consultant came in and studied the current processes. The consultant recommended that Robert could reduce one staff person and exceed current quantity and quality standards if a new process was implemented. Robert had one vacant position in his team, and he was quite certain that the consultant was making this recommendation so Robert wouldn't be able to fill the position. The consultant did recommend that the group not fill the position. Robert was angry and frustrated. He knew his business and didn't need an outsider to come in and tell him how to do it better. Robert went to his group and expressed his anger. He told his team that he wasn't going to let anyone tell him how he should run his business. He told the group he was sure that not only would they not fill the vacant position, but that they would lay off additional employees. He added that the work this group performed has never been appreciated and never would be.

Robert's inability to manage his own feelings will play out in disastrous ways with his group. They will take on Robert's feelings, worries and beliefs and will not support the change implementation. Now, were Robert's feelings and perceived losses really based on what might happen? Maybe. Maybe not. But Robert needed to do his homework on his feelings so he could control them. He needed to reflect on his anticipated losses and feelings and work through them before talking to his employees and poisoning them.

So, let's do a retake. What could have Robert done instead?

Robert could have listened to the consultant in a thoughtful way. He could have left the consultant meeting and talked with a trusted colleague, or with his leader, or just sat by himself for twenty minutes. He could have asked himself what he thinks might be lost in this recommended change. Was he worrying that he might lose additional staff? Was he feeling dismissed because his way of running the licensing process was being called inefficient? Were people thinking he was a lousy leader? He could have worked through his worries and feelings before meeting with his team. Maybe the new recommended process could work out better? Even though a vacant position was not being filled, maybe additional reductions weren't being planned out in a villainous attempt. Maybe by leading the group in this new process, he would be seen as a strong leader who can make effective changes. Robert could then go to his group in an honest and authentic way. He could tell them that the work the team did in the past was great and with some changes the group could even be more successful. He could tell the group that the vacant position wouldn't be filled, but it could be that the group could process more licenses more effectively and efficiently than before because the team was good at what they did.

Again, the first step of self-awareness is the identification of the leader's emotional responses and anticipated losses. Secondly, the leader needs to work through feelings by talking about them to a significant other or partner, a friend, a colleague, or others who can listen; or through self-reflection. Thirdly, the leader needs to sort through the losses and pain by considering if the identified losses are really going to happen or if they are based on fear. Then, the leader needs to ask problem-solving questions. What is my role in this change? Finally, the leader needs to understand that the change might indeed change more, and the leader needs to ask for input and ideas about the change.

Questions the leader might consider during self-reflection include:

- What skills do I need to implement this change?
- How might my role change?
- What can I do to make sure I am engaged in this change?
- What are some creative ways I can lead during this change
- What are the pros and cons about this change?
- Are my emotional responses due to the proposed changes or might I be resistant to the change because it is change? Is my mood based on reality or my fears?
- How could my mood affect my team? If my mood did spread to others, how would that look?
- How can I genuinely consider new change ideas and listen to others' ideas?
- How could I present the change opportunity to staff so they can see possible pros?

Only through self-reflection, deliberate problem-solving questions, a conscious understanding that the change will probably change in some manner, and the leader's genuine interest in listening to change ideas, can the leader manage themselves in a way necessary to lead change.

# Chapter 7: Change Motivation

Change Motivation, the fourth competency of this framework, deals with the leader's commitment to achieve and meet excellence. Does the leader align himself or herself with the goals of the organization? Does the leader have initiative, and is the leader optimistic? All these questions are important for leaders in supporting and motivating themselves and others during change.

An effective organizational change leader is committed to the goals of the organization. It means that the leader needs to know the goals and needs to be committed to them, and he or she needs to be a positive leader.

Learning the goals of the organization might seem like a fairly easy task compared to trying to feel positive when one doesn't. Learning the objectives, goals and the vision of the organization typically means reading about the organization. However, sometimes during change, the goals of the organization may be changing as well. Sometimes leaders can get locked into what "used to be" and can't consider the future. Sometimes the stated goals related to the change don't happen until after the change is made. Being committed to the organization means that one needs to acknowledge that the organization is in flux, and not be hung up on what the organization used to be. I worked with an aerospace company that manufactured aerospace parts and subcomponents. When the organization made a business decision to slow the manufacturing of aerospace parts and instead moved forward to manufacturing medical devices, the management team was resentful and angry. The disgruntled leaders who could not embrace the change, and thus could not lead the change, were leaders who were committed to the existing product line rather than being committed to the organization and understanding the need for the organization to change and adapt. Those leaders who thrived in this company were people who were committed to the organization prior to the change, during the flux, and supported the decided direction the company was taking. Leaders who know the goals of the organization, who understand the organization's need to change, and who can be open to the new direction will lead better.

Being optimistic or positive during change is imperative for leaders. Many leaders ask me how they can stay positive when they believe the company is making a wrong move with the decided change. I find myself asking these leaders to tell me why the change decision is a poor one. Usually, I find that the leader is not open to the change and not interested in considering the change. Usually the leaders are experiencing loss of some kind and have not done the self-reflection work to discover what they think they might lose or gain from the change. By unpacking their anticipated losses and possible gains, leaders can engage in some thought about why the change might work and might be a good direction for the company. Regardless of where the leader "lands" regarding the change, in order for the leader to successfully lead the change, the leader has to be open and positive towards the new way.

The leader can engage in a reflective change activity to discover how the change could actually be good. Asking themselves the following questions after identifying feelings and potential losses can help them to be more receptive to change:

- Why is this change happening?
- What are the possible positive outcomes of this change for the company?
- What are the obstacles to this change? How could the obstacles be addressed?

- How could this change help me grow?
- How could this change help employees grow?
- How could this change create another career pathway?
- What new skills could I develop resulting from this change?
- How is this change better than what's been done before?
- How could the company actually prosper from this change?
- How can I show to the people I lead through what I say, how I behave, and my mood, that I am open to this change?
- How can I show to my colleagues and upper leadership through what I say, how I behave, and my mood, that I am open to this change?

When leaders are committed to their organizations (even when they know that they won't work there forever) and are committed to its evolution and are open to the change, they are tremendously more successful at implementing change. By engaging in self-reflection and asking oneself questions, the leader will become more positive, engaged and committed to the organization, and more successful in leading the change process.

# Chapter 8: Social Awareness

The fourth leg of CLEI, Change Social Awareness, is where the leader empathizes and understands what his or her employees are feeling as part of the change. Does the leader coach the employees to help listen to their pain, and the feelings and losses that the employees might experience as part of the change? Or does the leader ignore the employees and use primarily command-and-control leadership?

Just as it is important to have empathy for his or her followers, it is just as important for the leader to demonstrate empathy for his or her managers that lead others. Let's start with the followers.

## Empathy with Followers

Many leaders don't empathize with the employees at all. They believe that the employees should just do their job and not be distracted with all the drama or emotions that employees bring. They keep the focus on only work tasks and try to manage emotions away. By ignoring how people are feeling, leaders are not solving any problems or decreasing resistances to change. Leaders need to be aware of employees' emotions and be able to move the employees in positive directions. Leaders can't do this by ignoring their employees, avoiding them, playing hush-hush, or discounting the emotions they are experiencing. Leaders need to care. The neuroscience research supports that in order to build effective leadership relationships and to help staff feel motivated and willing to change, that leaders need to be empathic and care [19]. Inherent in the STAMP (Storytelling, Taking a breath, Active listening, Mood and Morale evaluation, and Problem-solving) coaching method, later described in this book, leaders can effectively and easily provide an experience between the employee and the leader where the employee can reflect on his or her feelings and the leader can empathize. Some easy questions to start the conversation might include:

- How do you feel about this?
- What do you think you might be losing or gaining from this change?

As stated earlier—just as it is important to have empathy for their followers, it is important for leaders to have empathy for their leaders.

## Empathy with Leaders

Change leadership isn't just about leading the followers; it is about supporting and leading the upper leadership. "Managing up" becomes a key activity that good change leaders do. Regardless of where you are as a leader in the organization, you likely have an upper leadership structure. Those leaders and influencers are not without anticipated losses, grief and pain. They too are getting direction from others, and they need to be supported in the change event. They need support in understanding that the change may evolve. They need support in being positive. If your leadership is not positive and open to the evolving change, they cannot lead or support others.

When your leaders engage with you about their frustration, anger and disappointment, you have a decision to make. You can allow their emotional vomit to stick on you or you can be emotionally intelligent enough to be supportive of your boss but not be dragged in the trenches of negatively and not let your boss remain there. You have an opportunity to demonstrate your keen ability to lead effectively in change. You can be the optimal leader of change by not only leading others in change but by supporting your leadership team as well. Engaging with your leaders to ask questions and engage in conversation that offers positive support and encouragement will support them to be open to the change, to embrace the commitment of the organization, and ultimately to support you. Being authentic in this kind of leadership will be noticed by all favorably.

So, if the leader is extraordinary in being self-aware, self-managed, motivated, and empathetic, can that leader be an effective leader? Although these emotional intelligence legs are key to good leadership, the leader cannot stop here. Without the final leg of Change Social Management skills, the leader will be ineffective.

# Chapter 9: Change Social Management

Change Social Management, the final competency leg of CLEI, is an attribute of a leader who can effectively help the employees to move positively forward to implement and sustain the change. How does the leader communicate? How often? When? And can the leader effectively coach employees, colleagues and leaders to assist them in actually engaging and are embracing the change? Has the leader written a change leadership plan that engages employees? Does the leader coach in a manner where employees are discovering their roles and are engaging in their own problem-solving? Can they effectively manage change through collaboration and cooperation, and create team synergy?

Using the STAMP coaching strategy (Chapter 14) when interacting with followers and with other leaders is an effective method of helping others move forward during change. This model includes a significant step in facilitating problem solving where the employee is actually engaged in solving problems. The STAMP method provides a framework where the coaching session provides the opportunity for the leader to empathize and help the employee move forward.

In addition to STAMP coaching, the leader will choose other effective change strategies such as communicating effectively, helping employees find their "fit" in the change, explaining the vision, recognizing employees and other strategies. All of these activities require deliberate consideration in helping employees move forward and embrace change positively.

This leg of emotional intelligence is probably the most complex and requires the most skill from change management leaders. It requires the leader to be evaluative of the organization's emotional landscape, the organization's readiness for change, the complexity of the change(s),and the degree of strength the leaders at all levels bring, and to be thoughtful in playing out what strategies will bring the most return on investment. Some people think that just being aware of their own and others' feelings is enough emotional intelligence. It isn't—it is a mistake. If a leader feels for people, and empathizes but doesn't help support them with moving forward with the change, it is actually destructive. It is destructive to the employee because inadvertently you may be allowing them to lie in emotional vomit. Worse yet, listening to employees' feelings, and empathizing fully without supporting forward movement and problem solving, will result in you too lying in sickening vomit that leaves you unable to implement the change.

# Section 3: Change Management Strategies

So, what are the strategies for effectively implementing change? Yes, you have to have CLEI to use the strategies; it is a given. CLEI helps inform the leader in choosing the appropriate change strategies. The strategies are not prescriptive in that you use them like a cookbook. You have to know when and how to use them. Every organizational culture is unique. Every leader brings different skills. The emotional landscape of a culture is constantly changing.

Writing a project management plan is often a recommended course in implementing change. Any significant change event should include the writing of a project management plan. That being said, leaders must also write an intentional change leadership plan, or the project management plan must include change leadership strategies.

When the leader is using CLEI principles, the leader is able to identify when and how he or she should facilitate visioning and role "fitting"; communicating, motivating, recognizing, celebrating, coaching and training; building effective teams; leading with the most effective style; evaluating the change; writing effective change management plans and remaining positive and caring for themselves.

This section addresses effective change management strategies and how to use them.

# Chapter 10: Visioning

Visioning addresses and alleviates losses in positive outlook, belonging, security, trust, and leadership support.

## Pre-Test: How is your organization doing?

Indicate your level of agreement using the scale **1—Strongly Disagree, 2—Disagree, 3—Agree, 4—Strongly Agree.**

1. The organization has a clear vision/mission.
2. The organization's vision/mission is shared often.
3. The organization has written a "change event" vision statement.
4. The "change event" vision statement is shared frequently.
5. The "change event" vision includes the "what," "why," "how," "hope," employees' roles, acknowledgement of emotions and a call for commitment.

*Score:*

*Key:*

*19 or above – Exceptional*

*15 to 18 – Good with development opportunities*

*13-14 – Needs improvement*

*Below 13 – Need to address immediately*

Visioning allows employees to feel secure within the organization. It addresses the loss issues that employees may experience around feeling insecure and a lack of belonging. They know where the organization is going. They have a vision and a purpose. It gives employees a sense of direction. Without a change vision, people feel helpless and think they are victims. With a vision, they are committed, have purpose, and are loyal. They figure out how they fit in, and they support the organization. Visions must also include hope—even when the message is dismal. A leader shouldn't misrepresent the change, but should be deliberate in finding some kind of authentic hope in the message. The vision must be repeatable and be repeated. It should be delivered in all-hands meetings, team meetings, during one-on-one coaching sessions as well as via email, newsletters and other communication means. Whenever possible, using a kick-off event to describe a new vision is a great way to share the vision, to help people understand the change is real, and to put some happiness around that new vision.

During the kick-off, make sure you recognize the hard work that has been done in the past. Often leaders try to villainize the former way things were handled or processes done as a method of getting employees excited about the new change. By talking poorly about the old processes, procedures or products, or by dismissing all that was done by employees prior to the change, employees will become disengaged and will feel unvalued.

So, what is that vision statement of change? It spells how and why the change is needed, how it will be implemented, and how each employee can support it. It is clear, concise, and speaks the truth in a passionate way. It has to be passionate to draw commitment and support. It cannot be boring and lack commitment. It can't be too complicated such that employees can't remember its contents. The elements of a vision include:

✓ the what
✓ the why
✓ the how
✓ the hope
✓ the role of employees

✓ acknowledgement of emotions

✓ and a call for commitment

*Tips:*

- Talk about the change and organizational vision frequently.
- Be authentic when describing the change.
- Be passionate and use many descriptive words.
- Be prepared for questions and discussions. Don't be defensive. Be open.
- Talk about the vision "sooner than later". Remind people it might evolve.

Mapping out the vision before the leader shares the change is important. The vision-creating must be intentional and thoughtful. Whenever possible, the leader should include others in the vision development. When the leader includes others, employees will be invested in the change. Vision creation with others will usually result in developing some early adopters or ambassadors of the change. Although sitting down with others via a focus group, retreat, or other meeting takes time, the return on investment will be seen quickly. Sometimes, because of the already given directive or lack of time, the leaders cannot develop the vision statement with others and must write the statement by themselves or with other leaders.

Covering each element of a vision statement is important and should be described at a higher level. Start with the "what." What is going to change? Is there going to be a...

- Downsizing?
- Reorganization?
- Change in product line?
- Service delivery reconfiguration?

- Relocation?
- Change in physical seating?
- Process improvement or continuous improvement implementation?

Describe the change in one or two sentences, being honest, accurate and concise.

The second element, the "why", needs to succinctly indicate why the change is needed. Examples of why the change is needed might include:

- It is a needed cost saving.
- It will bring more efficiencies.
- The organization will be more sustainable.
- It is meeting customer or stakeholder requirements.
- It will increase productivity.
- Funding has been cut.
- Leadership (including the board of directors, board of trustees, stockholders, elected or owners) has another direction.
- It will increase quality.

The third element, the "how", should be explained in a higher-level way and must be authentic. If the "hows" might include input from employees, then say it. If the how has been already determined by others, don't pretend that input is welcome. The "hows" may include:

- A consultant will be coming in to make recommendations.
- Each of you will be asked for input and recommendations.
- It will be a phased-in process over the next six months.
- Customer input will be used.
- Employees manufacturing the identified outsourced product will be laid off, or the least senior will be laid off.
- A team will be created with a charter to direct activities.
- A project manager will be hired.

- Training will be provided in phases.

The roles of employees, whether specific or higher level, should be delineated in the statement. The more specific role description will bring investment into the work. However, sometimes the role of the employees isn't clear yet. Or there are so many individual roles that the leader cannot speak to all of them. Whatever the situation, the vision statement must somehow indicate the importance of employees' roles. Examples might include:

- Employees currently doing product technical support will also be providing support of customers as well.
- Technicians will be counted on to provide their input.
- Employees will be doing more grant development work and less client service work.
- Employees will be looking at their own work processes and will be recommending cost savings methods.

The element of "hope" must be authentic and can be tricky. It must be honest but cannot be overstated. Examples of hope statements might include:

- By making these cuts, the company can expect to be more sustainable and can remain competitive.
- By giving up offices, we expect that teams can be more collaborative.
- By taking on this new process/product, we believe employees will gain new skills with provided training.
- Even though we are downsizing employees, we will be providing them with resume development and placement services.
- By taking on this new product line, we believe that we will be more competitive.

Although we won't directly be providing this service anymore, we will still provide other valued services to our clients.

Another essential element to be included in the vision statement includes the acknowledgment of hard work and the expectation of emotional responses. Those comments might include:

- We realize people will be sad to see some of their colleagues leave.
- We know that it can be frightening to work in different markets.
- It will probably be an adjustment for all of us when using this new process.
- It is expected that some of you may be worried about the future.
- You may be feeling overwhelmed.
- Change can be hard on people, and you may feeling anxiety or stress over these changes.

Finally, the vision statement must call out for the commitment of employees, either through a general higher-level need or specific needs. Examples might include:

- We need every one of you to help us implement this new product line.
- We are depending on each of you to be part of the planning process.
- We are asking each of you to participate in training so you can use this new technology.
- This means that each of you will need to work together in your new teams.

# Chapter 11: Role "Fitting"

Role fitting addresses and alleviates losses in security, identity, belonging and competence.

## Pre-Test: How is your organization doing?

Indicate your level of agreement using the scale **1—Strongly Disagree, 2—Disagree, 3—Agree, 4—Strongly Agree.**

1. The organization deliberately outlines any role changes as a part of a "change event".
2. The organization makes sure each employee knows how his or her role has changed.
3. The organization facilitates a needs assessment to determine what types of training needs to be addressed.
4. Each employee knows how their role supports the "change event".
5. Employees' roles are discussed during coaching sessions.

*Score:*

*Key:*

*19 or above – Exceptional*

*15 to 18 – Good with development opportunities*

*13-14 – Needs improvement*

*Below 13 – Need to address immediately*

Many leaders complain about employees wanting to know their role or how they fit in. Managers often are heard to say "They are just lucky to have a job." Most leaders think that employees will intuitively know or figure out their roles independently. Employees don't. Most people do create narratives about what their role might involve, but is often a negative narrative including themes of displacement, layoffs, etc.

When employees don't know their roles in the change implementation, and don't know how they fit in, they don't feel like they belong and don't feel secure. If they don't feel like they belong, they won't be motivated to work at the highest level. They step all over each other, trying to grasp their place in the organization. Unfortunately, if employees are not feeling valued and are unclear of their roles, they will not only lack motivation and perform at a lower level, but will spread negativity in the organization or company. Employees may even be likely to sabotage the change event. Employees at all levels need to know their purpose and how they fit within the organization. If they know their roles, they will be valued, secure and know that they belong.

The earlier that "role-fitting" discussions and clarity can be provided, the better. Whether it is the leader, manager, or employee without authority, discussions should be facilitated to determine what roles will remain constant, what roles might change, and which employees will be performing various roles. In addition to looking at role changes, some structural changes may need to be made based on customer requirements, changed processes and other changes.

Often, role mapping and road mapping is contracted out with a change expert or facilitated by an internal employee who has some organizational development background. Role mapping is one method where the facilitator can begin to look at roles and provide clarity. Whenever possible, it is important to include employees in these discussions. Whereas role mapping delineates each employee's role, road mapping helps employees see how their function and role supports the organization. Skilled facilitation using CLEI must be used to frame and lead the discussion. The facilitator must:

- Convey that all previous work has beenvalued, as well as the work the employees will be performing. Employees need to know that they have been valued and will continue to be valued.
- Ask the group to look for opportunities with role changes, be willing to remain fluid, and be positive.
- State the change vision and purpose, listing the purpose and priorities of the change.
- Define how success might be measured. If those measurements are known already, they should be described in detail.
- Assist the team in listing needed functions, responsibilities and roles. Those functions should include current functions that will remain, as well as identifying the new functions required.
- Align functions and roles with employees through discussion.
- Demonstrate how each role supports the priorities and outcomes of the organization. By doing this, employees will feel a sense of belonging.
- Identify any additional training that should be considered. Does the person performing a new role or new tasks need training? How can that be determined? How will that be structured, and how will that be communicated? By addressing the training needs, many employees' feelings of loss of competency will be addressed.

During a traditional role mapping exercise, the facilitator often identifies current positions and clearly identifiable work for each position. The facilitator then works with others to identify needed changes to roles resulting from the change event. New skills, processes and techniques are identified. See Appendix A for a description of a possible road mapping exercise. If the proposed change is transformational in nature, it may make more sense to start with the customer or system requirements and map future roles first. If the organization uses Lean value stream mapping as a visualization tool for recording processes, the value stream mapping can be used as a starting point to identify specific functions. Visual mapping or streaming – whether with flip charts, diagrams or other representations – should be used as a way to document what is being considered, identified and agreed upon. By using visual representations, the facilitator and others can visualize linkages, requirements and the need to further define roles. After roles have been clarified and employees are assigned to those roles, a training and development inventory needs to be used to identify areas of needed development.

Communication of possible role changes, as well as the reassurance that the organizational leadership values each employee, should be shared at the onset of the anticipated change. Employees need to be included in the role mapping process whenever possible. Medium to large organizations may not be able to include all employees, but should include some employees from all levels and teams. Once the roles and functions have been established, this information should be communicated quickly to avoid rumor mills. It is recommended that roles be depicted in writing for employees, so that employees can clearly state how their specific role supports the organizational vision, priorities and outcomes.

*Tips:*

- Make sure someone in your organization, or a consultant, has reviewed roles to see if they have changed.
- Know how roles and functions have changed.
- Make sure each employee knows how their role supports the vision.
- Make sure a skills or behavior analysis has been facilitated to support training opportunities.

- Remind employees that they have an important and valued role in the change. Tell them they belong.

# Chapter 12: Communicating

Communicating addresses and alleviates losses in positive attitude, security, identity, belonging, trust and leadership support. Communication back and forth is important. Many organizations just stop talking during change.

## Pre-Test: How is your organization doing?

Indicate your level of agreement using the scale **1—Strongly Disagree, 2—Disagree, 3—Agree, 4—Strongly Agree.**

1. The organization tends to communicate the "change event" vision and details sooner rather than later.
2. Communication regarding the change occurs at all levels.
3. Many modalities of communication are used to talk about the change vision, process and other information; e.g. email, newsletter, all-hands meetings, one-on-one coaching, and visual presentations.
4. Employees are enlisted to communicate the change vision, process and other information.
5. Change "kick-offs" are frequently used to describe changes.

*Score:*

*Key:*

*19 or above – Exceptional*

*15 to 18 – Good with development opportunities*

*13-14 – Needs improvement*

*Below 13 – Need to address immediately*

During change, organizational silence may envelope the company. The literature suggests many organizations experience a phenomenon called organizational silence [6] [7] [8], where direct reports are not willing to speak up about issues, they withhold their opinions, and do not discuss the problems. Argyris and Schon [20]asserted that managers fear negative feedback because they might feel embarrassed or might see the negative feedback as a threat to their competence. Morrison and Milliken [6]believed managers' fear of negative feedback and their belief that employees are untrustworthy and interested primarily in themselves might create organizational silence, a condition that can be a potentially dangerous impediment to successful organizational change.

Leaders resist communicating honestly and openly to staff. They get busy, they are entrenched in planning, they don't trust employees with information, and they don't know how to communicate change in the most effective manner. Most leaders want to wait until the change is totally understood and can be articulated. This might be an ego issue for the leaders; they are in authority and want to be viewed as "all knowing." This mistake often breaks the trust between management and employees. Once that trust is broken, it is hard to build back.

When employees don't hear information and updates, they often engage in negative talk, speculating what might happen and consequently emotionally vomiting on each other. They create catastrophic and negative narratives and scripts that are repeated over and over again. Employees don't stand around the water cooler discussing how management is brilliant and that they know that they will be taken care of. Don't trick yourself with this belief. Instead they talk with each other, fabricating worst-case scenarios that only bring morale down and decrease employee engagement.

Communication is important because it helps people stay positive even when the news might be worrisome. They trust management and feel secure and feel like they belong. They will be more inclined to work hard, gossip less, and feel overall positively about the organization. Through repetitive messaging, employees know that the change is "real." It is critical that leaders understand the importance of communication, understand that it is not a just a "one-time thing", and that communication should sometimes be interactive. Not only is communication important for employees, it must be provided to internal and external customers and stakeholders. Often organizations will change processes or working conditions that affect customer experiences and/or set up angst with labor. Intentional and frequent conversation and dialogue must be executed in a way to include internal employees and stakeholders.

My experience has been that leaders will sometimes make an obligatory communication via email or during a hands-on meeting, but then the communication quickly ends. So, how much should a leader communicate? A leader should communicate regularly and early. If a change is being considered or is delayed, that should be communicated. The leader should inform employees and others if the change direction has evolved or is "on-hold". Regardless of the stage of the change, regular communications are essential and required.

*Tips*

- Communicate earlier rather than later.
- Ensure communication happens at all levels.
- Communicate through every modality: visually, auditory, and written.
- Invite employees from all levels to share communication about the change.
- Launch kick-offs to communicate change.

▪ Admit when there are roadblocks or uncertainty about the change.

Communication should take place in every modality. Emails are a great way to message visions and updates and expectations. All-hands meetings bring everyone together to hear the same message, and provide for an opportunity to talk with colleagues. Coaching sessions with employees allow the interactive dialogue that needs to happen for employees to embrace and implement the change. Focus groups and team discussions allow employees and leaders to consider ideas together. Change planning groups provide an opportunity for employees to feel included and be ambassadors of change. Continual ongoing communication involving leaders and employees is much more productive than an infrequent email that comes from leadership where employees develop their own possibly misguided narratives of the change.

What should be communicated in messages? Nearly all change communication messages, whether the messaging is in writing or face to face, should include core components:

✓ Vision or restated vision statements (including core components mentioned earlier).
✓ Details of change—possibility of additional changes.
✓ Role description, whenever possible.
✓ Hope and opportunity and reassurance.
✓ An invitation for more conversation and input.

The choice of who delivers the initial vision statement and ongoing communication updates needs to be intentional and strategic. Yes, leaders should be communicating frequently, and strategically it makes sense for employees from all levels be given the opportunity and responsibility to communicate as well. By sharing the communication activities, employees from all levels will become your ambassadors to change. In addition, employees often hear a message from a colleague and will give it more credibility because it came from a peer. So think intentionally about communication opportunities. During a kick-off event, it may make more sense to have several employees deliver messages with you, rather than you delivering the content independently.

# Chapter 13: Motivating, Recognizing and Celebrating

Motivating and recognizing employees with celebrating addresses and alleviates losses that occur in positive outlook, competence, territory, security, belonging and leadership support.

## Pre-Test: How is your organization doing?

Indicate your level of agreement using the scale **1—Strongly Disagree, 2—Disagree, 3—Agree, 4—Strongly Agree.**

1. The organization celebrates what has happened in the past before it celebrates the new.
2. The organization intentionally celebrates most change milestones.
3. Leaders from all levels acknowledge employees' good performance and change behavior.
4. Leaders praise supervisors' and managers' good performance and change behavior.
5. Recognition and praise is provided often.
6. Recognition and praise includes the following three elements: the recognized specific behavior, connection of behavior to effect, and the thank you.

*Score:*

*Key:*

*22 or above – Exceptional*

*18 to 21 – Good with development opportunities*

*15-17 – Needs improvement*

*Below 15 – Need to address immediately*

Leaders often dismiss the importance of recognition. What leaders miss is that there is a business case for recognition. Nelson reports that recognition and rewards are important because these activities actually drive organizational performance [21]. Sometimes leaders are so busy leading a change event, monitoring the progress, and setting new goals that they neglect the celebrations. Once a goal is met, there is a new goal, and the leader is concentrating on the new milestone. The leader eagerly launches the new milestone without recognizing the accomplishments of employees, and misses the opportunity to make the workplace fun.

Companies often believe they need a rewards and recognition program that requires resources to provide for big prizes and expensive trips. This is simply not true. Meaningful recognition is more important than token gifts or vacations given to just a handful of employees. Also, don't assume that motivating employees always means that you have to do a "canned" recognition program. Although motivating employees can happen through recognition and celebration, it is important to note that employees also comment that they are motivated when they feel like they belong to the organization, when they hear about what is going on, when they have challenging work, and when they are included in planning, decision-making, and implementation strategies. So, start with great communication and employee inclusion and opportunities for employee development. That being said, recognition and celebration has its place and can be very effective during change.

To ensure that employees are motivated, it is important that leaders recognize individuals, teams, and departments as well as celebrating accomplishments throughout the process. I met a leader who told me that when she was in the midst of change and was stressed, she turned "all business." Her demeanor was sullen, angry and curt. She was great at telling people what they should do and how to do it. She was amazing at setting milestones. She was so shortsighted that she couldn't see the importance of recognizing, encouraging and celebrating employees. Her employees didn't want to work for her, didn't support her, and sabotaged the change effort. Leaders must encourage and motivate employees. It is our job as leaders.

So, how do you motivate employees? I have watched countless times as leaders create "employee of the quarter" or "employee of the year" programs. These quick and easy recognition programs are ineffective and pointless. In fact, the remaining employees feel so disenfranchised that they were not recognized, that these types of recognition programs actually do more harm than good. If you are using these types of programs to motivate your employees, get rid of them.

Recognition and motivation are core elements of good change leadership. However, they are not easy. Recognizing and celebrating appropriately requires some thought. Without deliberately thinking through recognition, the leader may cause unintended consequences such as lowered performance and morale. Some quick thoughts about B.E.T. recognition model offered by the Maritz Institute using neuroscience underpinnings:

✓ B. Behavior- State the specific behavior observed or noted.
✓ E. Effect- Connect the behavior to the effect, and
✓ T. Thank you- Say "thank you" with sincerity. [22]

# Types of Recognition

Choices for types of recognition include the following:

## Individual acknowledgement and recognition

Individual recognition is one of the most effective ways to motivate employees. They feel valued and respected. Remember to use the B.E.T. recognition model [22]. When recognizing individuals, the leader should call out the specific work or behavior they did to implement the change. Don't rest on easy phrases such as "Great job, Ayesha." Instead think about what that employee did that really contributed to the change effort. Then, connect that behavior to the change effect. For example, "Ayesha, I heard how you supported your colleagues when they were having difficulty implementing the change, and I want to personally thank you for supporting the reorganization underway." Or, "Ayesha, I noticed how quickly you tried the new process and want to thank you for identifying the problems and new solutions- you helped us implement this new strategy in a timely fashion." Be strategic in how you offer praise. You can provide the praise in person, within a team setting, all-hands meetings, via an email, or through a written note. Remember to be clear about detailing the good behavior or performance and connecting the behavior to the change effect. And, don't forget to provide a sincere and earnest thank you.

### Tips

- Identify milestones and metrics.
- Celebrate each milestone.
- Recognize good performance and behavior every day.
- Be specific in recognizing the good behavior, connecting the "dots" to the change effect, and say a sincere thank you.
- Recognize individuals, teams and the organization.
- Be specific and timely when providing recognition and praise.
- Quit using employee of the month, quarter and year programs.

## *Team acknowledgement and recognition*

Whenever possible, acknowledge the entire team's performance. By acknowledging the team, you not only motivate the employee and show them that you value their work, but you share with the team that you value and support the team effort. Again, be specific and clear. Avoid saying, "Great work, team", and instead outline exactly what you valued from the team's work. Perhaps saying, "I am so impressed with how the team exceeded the quality standards on this new project by 9%." or "Although there have been many downsizing events in the last year, patients have reported continual satisfaction of their care." Be strategic in how you offer team praise. Praising the team together can build cohesiveness; following up in writing provides additional support and motivation to team members.

## *Larger organizational acknowledgement and recognition*

Larger organizational acknowledgement is an effective way to motivate larger groups and can help employees see how their role supports the larger organizational change event. Think carefully before calling out a specific individual in front of the larger group. Will this recognition motivate all staff, or do you think that it might alienate the larger group? Be deliberate and thoughtful when recognizing in larger groups. Certainly, when the organization and its parts have pulled together to implement the change event, it is very appropriate to recognize all the teams that worked together and accomplished great things that supported the change. Again, avoid saying, "What a great organization." or other meaningless recognition messaging. Instead be clear and detailed. Think ahead and strategize. Perhaps saying something such as:

*"Manufacturing this new product was a challenge. I appreciate the way manufacturing, engineering, quality control and our Lean experts worked together to exceed our manufacturing goals. Also, I want to acknowledge the sales team for representing our new product so well. Our shipping department expedited the parts out quickly to our customers, and our administrative staff supported all of us during this new product development. I appreciate your willingness and commitment to taking on a new product line that will keep this company sustainable."*

Celebrations should be coordinated often and during many phases of the change event. Coordinate or encourage others to plan potlucks, teambuilding, or other activities where employees can be recognized and can enjoy what has been done. These activities will serve as a motivation for continued outstanding performance. During the activity, the team should be thanked intentionally and a brief description of the next milestone should be introduced or described again.

# Chapter 14: Change Coaching Method: STAMP

The Change Coaching Method: STAMP addresses losses in positive outlook, security, competence, control, identity, belonging, trust and leadership support.

## Pre-Test: How is your organization doing?

Indicate your level of agreement using the scale **1—Strongly Disagree, 2—Disagree, 3—Agree, 4—Strongly Agree.**

1. Leaders from all levels coach their employees regarding the change.
2. Leaders from all levels contain their own personal negative responses and comments during coaching sessions.
3. Leaders from all levels listen intently without "jumping in" during discussions.
4. Leaders from all levels empower employees rather than micromanage employees.
5. Leaders from all levels discuss the change vision, process, details and employees' roles.
6. Leaders from all levels engage in problem-solving discussions where the employee is driving the solutions.
7. Leaders from all levels inspire hope and opportunity during coaching sessions.

*Score:*

*Key:*

*26 or above – Exceptional*

*22 to 25 – Good with development opportunities*

*18-21 – Needs improvement*

*Below 18 – Need to address immediately*

Coaching becomes one of the most critical activities a leader can use to facilitate change effectively. Coaching happens at many different levels and with many types of employee. Whether you lead front line employees, supervisors, managers, directors or others, you need to treat your coaching role as one of the most important activities you do. Whether you lead early adopters, naysayers, or other employees with varying degrees of resistance or acceptance, coaching is your tool to get that change moving.

So, what counseling and coaching strategies can we use to introduce change? First we need to get our arms around what happens when we introduce organizational change. Change is detected as an "error" in our brains—the error being the difference between expectation and actuality [11]. By introducing change, we actually create pain in people's minds. Employees are not, for the most part, resisting change because they are bad people; they resist change because it actually hurts. So, how do we change those mental maps that people have that tell them that the current way of doing business is the best? I have typically observed leaders making four fundamental mistakes when coaching: they just don't do it, they empathize too little, they empathize too much, and most often they tell the employee the solution. Let's look at each of these mistakes in turn:

# Mistake #1 – They don't do it

Leaders are busy. They are tired. They have competing priorities. They have to produce outcomes. They just don't have time or even the desire to coach employees. Employees are adults. They get paid. They should just do what they need to do, right?

Wrong. If leaders don't spend time with their employees, giving them support, those employees will not perform as well as the employees who are coached. Leaders cannot afford not to coach. If they don't "pay now," they will "pay later." Coaching doesn't mean that leaders need to sit down with an employee every day for an hour. It may be that the leader checks in just 10 to 20 minutes a week with an employee.

## Mistake #2 – They empathize too little

Many leaders don't empathize with the employee at all. They believe that the employee should just do his or her job and not be distracted with all the drama or emotions that other employees bring. They keep the focus on only work tasks and try to manage emotions away.

Biologically, we have emotions. Those emotions can eat logic for lunch. By ignoring how people are feeling, leaders are not solving any problems or decreasing resistances to change. Instead, they are creating an environment where employees' emotions can breed like rabbits. Leaders need to be aware of an employee's emotions and be able to move the employee in positive directions. Leaders can't do this by ignoring their employees, avoiding them, playing hush-hush, or discounting the emotions the employees are experiencing.

## Mistake #3 – They empathize too much

Many leaders have such strong negative feelings themselves about the change event that they actually fall into the trap with the employee. The employee articulates concerns and feelings that the leader also mirrors. Leaders find themselves acknowledging and feeling the same things as their employees. In fact, following the conversation, the leader and employee both walk away feeling more negative and resistant and defeated by the change. Through their exchange of negativity, both walk away with their brains cementing their negative assumptions and beliefs about the change.

Although it is important to listen to employees' feelings, acknowledge them, and offer support, it is so important that leaders effectively coach their employees to the opportunities within change. This means the coaching session cannot turn into a non-stop "bitch" session; it must include listening, understanding and empathizing, but then going to problem-solving. Leaders who invite their employees to non-stop complaining sessions only end up filling up their employees and themselves with a belief system that the change will be disastrous.

## Mistake #4 – They tell the employee the solution

The biggest mistake leaders make during change is trying to tell the employee every solution, problem-solving every obstacle, and disempowering the employee to make decisions. We as leaders just can't help ourselves most of the time. We like to jump in and do that command-and-control thing we feel we are so good at. However, directing our employees causes many unintentional consequences. First, the employees become disempowered. They do this thing called learned helplessness. They become so dependent on the leader that they don't necessarily implement the change and they don't feel empowered to ever improve the change. Second, they probably won't implement the change because they have not bought into the change, and they resist it. Third, the employee is often the subject matter expert on a particular process, and ignoring their solutions is a loss to the organization. Finally, taking away employees' control of their work usually results in poor morale and personal loss.

Whenever possible, leaders need to empower employees by engaging them in problem-solving.

Using STAMP coaching strategies during change results in a significant return on investment. Using STAMP actually can result in an effective change being made. Even if the change makes business sense, is a good change, and could result in higher levels of productivity, those leaders not using STAMP will probably not meet their targets. You as a leader cannot afford to ignore your employees. Using STAMP will increase the likelihood that the change will be implemented well and that you will demonstrate your ability to lead well during change.

## Storytelling of Change

The **STAMP** coaching fundamentals are Storytelling, Taking a Breath, Active Listening, Mood Evaluating, and Problem Solving. The fundamentals are not sequential. They do not necessarily happen in order, nor do they happen once and then the leader is finished.

Preparing for the coaching session requires the leader to know the story of change. Be able to articulate what the change will entail in a timely manner, why it is happening, and be able to talk to the employee about their role in the change. The vision and the anticipated process must be retold over and over again, like a story. With the discussion of the story, dialogue must be provided so that the employee can talk about his or her specific role to the change.

*Tips*

- Talk often about the change and what it means.
- Ask employees to explain the change and change implications.
- Talk about the employee's role in the change.

It is important that you begin to coach and communicate the change story at the change event's idea conception, and not wait. Most leaders are reluctant to talk with staff until they know all the details of a clearly defined change vision and process. Sometimes, they wait because they don't want to upset their employees with changes that may not happen as initially designed. Once they know the final vision and process, they plan to begin the discussions. Seriously, how many change events have you been involved with or led where the conceived change was perfect and actually ended up being what was implemented? Exactly! It just rarely or never happens. Change visions and processes usually evolve. Such thinking is flawed. First, the change event usually changes to some degree anyway, so waiting until you know everything about it will probably never happen. Also, delaying conversations about the change will only upset employees further. However, if the leader is bound to secrecy due to a pending merger or other change that must be kept quiet, the leader needs to keep that possible change under wraps.

An unexpected consequence of waiting for a clearly defined change vision before talking to staff is the employees' innate ability to spin stories with disastrous outcomes. Employees have likely already heard of the upcoming change, right? Most employees will develop a change story that is usually vile and debilitating, not because they are bad people but because they are worried about what they might lose as a part of the change. Leaders need to be able to describe the change as the change concept evolves. So, leaders need to talk about the change in a way that depicts the evolution of the change. Saying things like "This is how the change might look," "This is how the change looks now," and "I will make sure to let you know how the change may be evolving," should be a part of every coaching session. The key element here is that leaders need to be communicating back and forth with employees from the idea conception throughout the change process. The anticipated change should be described with all the details that are known and can be shared over and over again. This repetition will help the employee develop mental maps that include the change being described.

Second to depicting the change event, leaders need to be able to provide the justification for the change. Sometimes the rationale for change makes sense, sometimes it does to some degree, and sometimes it doesn't at all. In fact, you yourself might be perplexed about why the change is occurring. The good leader tries to answer the questions the best they can. Whenever possible think hard and long about the justification for the anticipated change. Be ready to talk about it. Don't assume people should know the rationale. Talk about the thinking around and behind the change. Even if you don't agree with the rationale, be positive. Don't feel like you need to know all the answers either. Throughout the discussion, the leader should remain positive; the leader must also be authentic. So, when questions are asked and the leader simply doesn't know the answer, the leader needs to remain positive but not pretend to know why the change is happening. Being positive but honest is important to any change process. The employee will appreciate the leader who is authentic and doesn't know all the answers rather than the leader who pretends to know all.

The leader needs to engage with the employee, ready to explore and describe the employee's role in the change. It is key that the employee knows how he or she fits in to the change. So, spend extra time prior to the coaching session thinking about how this employee fits into the change. Then, explore with the employee how he or she will have a meaningful and valued role in the change. It may be that you don't know if or how the employee will have a role in the change. Maybe you don't know enough about the details or maybe this employee might be laid off. Saying that you are not sure but you value what they bring to the organization – and assuring them that you will continue to have conversations to see how the employee's role evolves when more is known about the change – is good. During most changes, however, there is a role for the employee or a couple of possible roles for the employee. Make sure you discuss them with the employee. Don't hold back from engaging the employee in this discussion simply because you think the change and the implications of change are apparent. The employees need to trust their leader and trust that their leader values them. Questions that might be asked during this conversation include:

- Given these anticipated changes, what would you be interested in doing?
- How do you think your skills align with the changes?
- If you were to perform this role, what training or skill development would you need?
- How do you think your role would change?
- How could I support you in this new role?

## Taking a Breath

Leaders need to take that breath during coaching or engagement with employees. Taking a breath allows time for the leader to reflect how they can use Change Leadership Emotional Intelligence (CLEI) during the change engagement with the employee. The leader needs to reflect how they themselves feel about the change, think about how they will manage their own emotions, consider how they will listen completely, and think about how they will help the employee move forward in the change event.

Considering how you feel about the change is critical. It is important that you know how you feel about the change and that you deal with your emotions before you engage with an employee. If you don't consider your feelings, and you choose not to deal with them, you may inadvertently emotionally vomit on your employee and create negative emotional contagion. A quick reminder regarding Achor's [18]work about mirror neurons and emotional contagion is worth repeating. Our emotions can infect a group of people in a moment! Your emotions are critical to your group of employees, colleagues or others. Employees will quickly take on what you are feeling. Thus it is important to know how you are feeling and have some control about what you express.

So, ask yourself the following questions. How do you feel about the change? Are you mad, frustrated, happy, irritated, cynical, or indifferent? Why do you feel this way? What might be some things that you might lose in the change? Have you lost your positive outlook, your sense of security, your ability to control your work, your identity and status, your territory, trust in management or a general lack of support for you as a leader in your organization? You are totally normal if you feel many or most of these losses. You need to recognize them and deal with them before you talk to your employees or you will infect them with your losses. Are you eating right? Sleeping right? Do you have a support system outside of work? Are you exercising? Do you have an employee advisory service or does your health coverage provide for support and counseling? Don't ignore your feelings. Don't be intolerable at your home with your interpersonal relationships. Don't let your work affect your personal life. If it does, get emotional support, work through your feelings so you can be available for your employees. You cannot be supportive of them if you are mad, hostile, depressed or lethargic.

*Tips*

- Know how you feel about the change.
- Be in a place where you don't spread your negative feelings.

• Be present and not distracted by your email, phone or other thoughts.

In addition to knowing how you feel and managing your feelings, you as the leader have to be ready to engage with employees through active listening skills and supporting them in embracing the change. Questions you may ask yourself:

• How do you feel about this change?
• What do you worry you might gain/lose as a result of this change?
• How can you better take care of yourself?
• How can you get perspective?
• Where are your support systems?

## Actively Listening

Critical to effective coaching sessions are the basics of actively listening: non-verbal communication, use of open-ended questions, paraphrasing and involving your employee in problem-solving.

*Tips*

• Don't talk all the time.
• Don't daydream or wait eagerly for a place you can jump into the conversation with your ideas.
• Listen completely.
• Ask open-ended questions.
• Be present.

Being prepared to listen provides the foundations of supporting your employee during change. So often leaders talk, talk and talk so much. They like to tell the employee what to do, how to do it, and then tell them again. Effective change management actually involves the leaders being silent. What a counter -intuitive thought—sit still. Ask questions and listen fully without jumping in with interruptions and directions. So, be prepared to listen and let your non-verbal communication show you are interested and care. Provide suitable eye contact, nod, and be prepared to listen. There are no magic formulas in establishing rapport, demonstrating receptive body language and facilitating a conversation. Everyone is different. Everyone has different comfort levels, cultures and backgrounds. The very best gauge you can use to figure out what you should do is evaluating the other person. Do they like to sit farther away than other employees? How much do they look at you? Use these behaviors to figure out what you should do. If they don't give you eye contact, don't stare them down. If they use intermittent eye contact, you use the same.

The use of open-ended questions helps get your employee to engage with you in a way that actually means something. The reality is that most of us used closed questions instead of open-ended questions. Closed-ended questions are questions that can be usually be answered with a yes or a no. Examples of closed questions are: Will you do this change? Can you do your new role? You will go to this training, right? These are questions that will not serve to engage with the employee. Try simple open-ended questions instead. Examples are: Talk to me about how this change impacts you. How will you implement this new scope of work? What gets in your way about this change? How do you feel about this? What can you do to turn this around? Asking open-ended questions and following up with brief and meaningful paraphrases of what he or she said will help the employee to a better understanding. Paraphrasing isn't hard but seems awkward at first. When leaders start paraphrasing what the employee said, they often act as parrots trying to paraphrase every word. That is not necessary. Just paraphrase what you think they said in a quick summary. Then, you launch into the problem-solving that is outlined below. Here is the most important suggestion to you: do not try to solve the problem first. Let the employees solve their problems whenever possible.

Active listening techniques are great. You can hear the employee's narrative on what he or she thinks is happening, but you can't stop there. The effective STAMP coach needs to evaluate the employee's mood and identify morale issues.

# Evaluating Mood and Morale

During the coaching session, be prepared to talk about the emotional side of the change. I know I am asking you to get emotional, and for many of you that is difficult. People are usually uncomfortable with emotions, especially when emotions are negative. They try to avoid them and cast them away. Be brave and consider the emotions and the morale of your employees. Ask how they feel about the change. Let them talk. Keep in mind that your employees will likely not approach you with their feelings about the change. We are taught at an early age that it is not professional to talk about our feelings or emotions. We are taught that if we talk about our feelings then we are weak. So instead, we as human beings act like emotions and feelings don't exist. We try to hide them and mask them in analytical justifications to support why we are depressed, sad or mad. By masking emotions, we miss the opportunity to deal with them. Your employees will probably never come to you and tell you that they are experiencing a loss in territory or control. They are more likely to come to you and tell you just why the change proposal is stupid and that management is stupid. Engage with your employees. Be present with their emotions. Don't try to provide immediate solutions. Just listen. Think about what they are feeling and use active listening techniques and problem-solving strategies to help the employee move forward with the change. Questions you can use to intimate this discussion include:

- How do you feel about this?
- What do you think you might be losing as part of this change?
- What good things can come from this change?
- How do you think others are feeling about this?
- What can you do to make this easier for you?
- How can I support you?

Using active listening, and getting a sense of how the employee is thinking and feeling, are necessary and critical to understanding the space employees are in. However, stopping there and just listening to someone vent and talk about their feelings is not enough. The STAMP coach needs to facilitate problem-solving and identification of opportunity and hope.

*Tips*

- Ask employee how they feel.
- Ask about the team morale.
- Ask how you can support the employee.

# Problem Solving and Hope

Problem solving is critical to implementing the new change event. But here is the secret: don't try to be the first to offer the answer. Try instead to get your employee to engage in problem solving before you jump in. Yes, I know you have great solutions. However, here is the reality. If you direct your employee with your ideas and solutions, they probably won't embrace them. No matter how great your ideas and solutions are, no matter how brilliant they are, the employee will fight your ideas. Their brains will detect the change and will fight the new concept, idea, process and scope of work. That is why you should engage with the employee to find their own solutions whenever possible.

During coaching, it is probably necessary to set up some structure at the beginning of the session and throughout the coaching experience. It's suggested that you begin the session with some boundaries. For example, start with some statements that give parameters: "I want to hear your concerns about the change and your feelings about the change. Let's spend ten minutes talking about that, but what I really need is your expert help in identifying some solutions, so let's plan on spending the remainder of our time together on that. I might have to interrupt you sometimes to help us stay on course to the problem solving."

Employees need to come up with the ideas. There are several reasons you want your employees identifying and thinking through their own solutions. The first reason is that most manufacturing and now other occupational arenas (government, retail, etc.) are now implementing continuous improvement tools and techniques such as Lean, Kaizen and front-line improvement strategies. It makes sense that these tools are used because they work. They work more often when the solutions originate from the "bottom up," not the "top down." Get employees identifying their own problems and wanting to identify more effective solutions for their own work. Second, when our brains have identified their own solutions and have created mental maps of how to perform in the jobs, we are more likely to implement the change. Let's face it, if we tell employees how to do their work, a lot of employees usually resist it. That is why it is imperative that we get our employees to find their own solutions. So resist the most tempting behavior of most leaders of offering our employees the solutions. Instead of telling, engage employees in their own problem solving. If you do, they will be more likely to follow through with the problem solving and actually implement the change. Make it a continuous practice. Ask questions. Hear their solutions. Explore those solutions with them. Follow up with them. Praise them for their ideas. Even if initially you don't know how the solutions could work. Don't shut them down.

A critical piece of the problem-solving component is that you must hold people accountable. Whether that is a metric that needs to be achieved by the employee or a problem-solving solution, it is critical that you write the agreement down and you revisit it. Let the employee know that you want him or her to update you during your next coaching session or via email, report, or other communication.

Some questions you might ask include:

- How do you think this can be fixed?
- What would it take you to turn this around?
- How would you solve this problem?
- What would you do?
- How could you help change the morale in our team?
- What would make you feel better?
- What would make you more engaged?
- What is a better way of doing this work?
- What would be the pros and cons of this solution?
- How could this risk be mitigated?
- What may be some skills/tasks you need to learn to do this job? How could you learn them?
- How could you make the new move to the new location feel comfortable?
- What are the challenges to this change? How could we address or solve these problems?
- How could you fix these problems?
- How could we better communicate this?
- How could we help employees embrace the change?

As an integral part of the problem-solving discussion, the STAMP coach must help the employee identify opportunities and hope that is inherent in the change. Creating opportunities and instilling hope will motivate the employee but must be authentic and meaningful. Sometimes finding meaningful opportunity and authentic hope in change situations is challenging. Perhaps the employee is being demoted, or perhaps the employee will no longer get to perform the work they love. Hope should not be disingenuous; the discussion needs to be realistic. It really isn't the leader's role to identify the hope but to help the employee identify hope. By empowering the employee to identify opportunities, the opportunities are more likely to be relevant to the employee. Consider using the following template to facilitate a coaching session with employees to identify hope, opportunity and solutions.

| Change Components | Loss? | Gain? | Challenges | Opportunities | Solutions or Actions | Support Needed for Self and through Others |
|---|---|---|---|---|---|---|
|  |  |  |  |  |  |  |
|  |  |  |  |  |  |  |
|  |  |  |  |  |  |  |
|  |  |  |  |  |  |  |

Or, consider using the following quadrant template to facilitate the discussion.

## Change or Change Component: _____

| Possible Losses | Possible Gains |
|---|---|
| | |
| Possible Solutions or Needed Activities | Support Needed |
| | |

*Tips*

- Share with your employee the expectation that they participate in problem solving.
- Resist temptation to jump in with solutions and provide advice.
- Help employee identify how change could bring opportunities to them professionally.
- Use questions and consider using diagrams or visuals to initiate the conversations.

Some questions you might ask include:

- As a part of this change, what are some new skills you might learn?
- How would this change help you grow and develop?
- How would this change create new opportunities to work and network with people?
- How would your new role create new possibilities?

# Special Coaching Circumstances

There are special coaching circumstances that we as leaders need to be mindful of. We need to consider the special needs of, and strategies for, early adopters, naysayers, toxic employees and leaders.

## Early Adopters

Early adopters of change are those employees who may be more accepting of change and/or someone who really likes and embraces the anticipated or implemented changes. You know who they are in your organization. You count on them. They are positive and have a good attitude.

Be prepared to spend more time rather than less time with early adopters. Early adopters are your ambassadors of change. However, to assume that they won't be negatively impacted by others' negative emotions and concerns is naive. Even your most positive employees can be impacted by others' fears and worries. Plan to individually and sincerely recognize early adopters.

## Naysayers

Naysayers make change implementation even more of a challenge than it already is. You know who they are. Those employees usually see the glass "half-empty." They see all the problems and challenges but can't see the hope and opportunity in the change. Naysayers need coaching and special care. They bring the risk of poisoning others and you with negativity.

Transitioning the naysayer to a positive ambassador role during the change might be one of the best strategies you can undertake to facilitate positive implementation of the change. Coaching this employee and including this employee in other planning groups could become one of the most positive things you can do.

## Toxic Employee

Toxic people are everywhere at the workplace. Most naysayers are not toxic but can be. Toxic people are those people with very difficult personalities. You know who I am talking about. Each of you probably has at least several. They might be passive aggressive, exhibit bullying behavior, are overly angry, or sabotage often. You must be willing to hold them accountable to a standard of good behavior. Talk to them honestly about their behavior and ask them first to identify what good behavior might look like. If they are unable to identify good behavior, then you state what that might look like and revisit the behavior during every coaching session. It is important that you do not allow a toxic person to sabotage the important change event. If coaching doesn't work, you need to visit your human resources or Employee Assistance Program (EAP) professional. Do not ignore bad behavior.

## Supervisors and Other Leaders

When you are supervising other leaders, your coaching sessions will be similar to coaching an employee without direct reports, except you will need todo more. In addition to learning about their feelings, mood, thoughts and helping them with problem solving, it is imperative that you state your expectation that they coach their employees and hold them accountable. By asking your leaders regularly, "How are your employees doing?" "How is coaching your employees regarding this change working?" "How often are you meeting with your employees?" and "How are you making sure that they are generating their own solutions to problems?" You need to hold your leaders accountable. By listening carefully to their responses, you will be able to evaluate if the leaders are coaching adequately, if they are supporting their employees, and if they are empowering their staff. Leaders can use this information to better coach other leaders in the organization. Perhaps you need to spend more time with this leader, write out expectations of coaching, and send the leader to change management training.

# Chapter 15: Facilitating Inclusion

Facilitating Inclusion addresses and alleviates losses in positive outlook, security, control, territory, belonging, trust, and leadership support.

## Pre-Test: How is your organization doing?

Indicate your level of agreement using the scale **1—Strongly Disagree, 2—Disagree, 3—Agree, 4—Strongly Agree**.

1. Leaders frequently involve employees during change planning meetings.
2. The organization routinely communicates updates and progress regarding the change event.
3. Employees are frequently included in the writing of project management and change leadership plans.
4. Employees are asked for their opinionsand ideas, and are encouraged to participate in "change event" dialogues.
5. Employees are asked to identify challenges and possible solutions during change.
6. Leaders are cognizant that marginalized people may already feel like they don't fully belong, and should address this through strategies and activities.

*Score:*

*Key:*

*19 or above – Exceptional*

*15 to 18 – Good with development opportunities*

*13-14 – Needs improvement*

*Below 13 – Need to address immediately*

It is dangerous not to include employees from all levels and all areas in planning groups and committees during every aspect of the change. If employees aren't included throughout the process, they will become disengaged. They will not work in productive ways, they will find reasons to resist the changes, and some will even sabotage the event.

The leader must make intentional decisions about employee involvement and inclusion. Many leaders come from a mentality that when change is implemented, it is something that we "do to" people rather than "do with" them. Many leaders scoff at this concept of inclusion and believe that they need to demonstrate their leadership through "showing people their authority." I am not suggesting that leaders give away their authority or power; I am asking instead that they include staff on decisions, planning, implementing and evaluating whenever possible. Including staff doesn't mean you give the entire change effort to employees and wish them well with it. It means that solid change leaders involve employees in the change planning and implementation process. It means they listen to employees, hear their concerns, ideas, and solutions. Leaders are not bound to what employees offer or concerns they might express. However, exceptional change leaders consider their thoughts, feelings, and ideas seriously and then make decisions based on sincerely hearing employee insights.

So, when do you include employees? The "earlier the better" and "more often than not" is the general rule. How can you include them? You can include them in a number of ways and have many choices.

It is important, when discussing inclusion, to consider the impact of marginalization of people during organizational change. The term "marginalized people" refers to various non-white ethnicities, spirituality groups, first generation cultures, women, people with disabilities, or other groups of people that are ignored. Marginalization results in a failure for the individual to achieve potential within society. [23]. The writings suggest that there are groups of people who do not have a sense of belonging in the workplace, even in the absence of any significant organizational change. To not acknowledge this reality and to not address this would be remiss. African-American women, for example, may still see themselves as being marginalized work players in their companies. They may feel as though they are not welcome and that they are outsiders [24]. If non-white ethnicities and other groups do not possess a feeling of belonging even when there have not been any layoffs or significant changes in personnel, one might suspect that their feelings of belonging to the organization would be further compromised during organizational change. Yuval-Davis [25] wrote about the notion of belonging, and the politics of belonging. Belonging is described as the emotional attachment or that feeling of being safe within an organization.

I often hear leaders say "I treat everyone the same", "I don't see a person's color or race", and "I'm not a racist". However, if you haven't explored the concept of white privilege, this might be an excellent opportunity to do some exploration. In a nutshell, white privilege is something that most white people don't even know they have, but do. White people have more privilege than others. Peggy McIntosh, a women's-studies scholar, started writing about the concept of privilege [26]. In her paper called "White Privilege and Male Privilege: A Personal Account of Coming to See Correspondences Through Work in Women's Studies", McIntosh described white privilege as an invisible weightless knapsack of assurances, tools, maps, guides, codebooks, passports, visas, clothes, compass, emergency gear, and blank checks. These privileges help Caucasians function well in our culture, society and work places. Whereas Caucasians take these assurances and tools for granted, marginalized employees may not. As effective leaders it is important to acknowledge that not all individuals may feel like they have that "knapsack" of assurances, tools and codebooks to navigate during change. And, it is critical that we make every employee feel supported, safe and engaged so that they have a sense of belonging within the organization. Make sure that all employees are involved in planning, decision-making, and implementing change. Make sure all employees are coached, recognized and respected. As leaders we need to encourage and support all of our employees.

*Tips*

- Find opportunities to include staff in planning, implementing and monitoring change at every opportunity.
- Include employees in the development of change management and project management plans.
- Ask employees for their help in sharing the change vision or message during all-hands meetings, team meetings or other communication venues.
- Tell people individually and collectively that they "belong".

# Regular communication

A relatively easy way to keep employees involved in change is regular communication from leadership. This can be accomplished through a weekly update email that is widely distributed. Make sure that communication happens every day and during every opportunity possible. Ineffective leaders think that they can announce the change once and be "done with it".

# Focus groups

Focus groups can work particularly well when you have specific issues or challenges inherent in the change process. Using focus groups, the leaders can hear brainstorming for possible obstacles and solutions directly from staff.

Starting with ground rules can help the discussion. Examples of ground rules might include:

✓ Respect
✓ Turn taking
✓ Timekeeping
✓ Requirement that a solution needs to be explored whenever a problem is identified

Although the leader, of course, is not bound to employees' suggestions or solutions, the leader still listens carefully to issues and uses ideas for planning implementation. Some examples of questions that may be used during the focus group include:

✓ What is your reaction to the change?
✓ What do you think the organization and you might lose from the change? Gain from change?
✓ What are the opportunities of this anticipated change?
✓ What are the challenges of this change?
✓ What are some of the solutions that could address the challenges?
✓ What would you recommend leadership do/consider when implementing this change?
✓ How can you support the organization during this change?
✓ Do you have other recommendations?

The above questions are a great way to begin a dialogue, but it is also important that someone facilitates the discussion. Make sure there are time parameters attached to each question. If the discussion is not facilitated and/or time is not being monitored, the discussion could easily turn into a gripe session with no positive outcomes or strategies. It is important that employees are asked what they feel and what they might lose/gain; however, the conversation cannot stop there. A good strategy while facilitating discussions is to use a white board with two columns: "challenge" and "possible solution".

## Staff or team meetings

Facilitating regular staff or team meetings is an excellent way for employees to be involved and included in change discussions. Some of the best change leaders will put the change event as a standing topic on their regularly scheduled meetings. As with focus groups, just having a topic and free-flowing discussion is not always the best way to include staff. Sometimes, totally free-flowing discussions turn quickly into complaint sessions, helping no one. Instead the team leader should frame the conversation with an update or status report on change, followed up with questions asking, "What is working well?" "What are challenges?" and "What are ideas or solutions to address problems?" Other successful leaders will begin a conversation with "OK, let's talk about concerns for ten minutes, and then we will talk about what is working right and possible solutions for the remaining twenty minutes." Good questions or statements might include:

✓ Give me a status on your work.
✓ Describe the challenges/possible solutions.
✓ How can you support your other team members during this change?
✓ What should we all be considering?

By structuring meetings in this way, employees understand that their feelings and emotions are important, but they are expected to participate in identifying opportunities and finding solutions. Employees will leave these facilitated meetings feeling heard and empowered to make change happen. They will also understand the expectation that the change will be implemented.

# Planning meetings

Whenever possible, establish and sustain planning meetings to create a project management plan or tackle a specific part of change implementation. Invite not only the employees with generally positive attitudes, but invite some of the naysayers as well. Remember that by including those naysayers in planning, they will usually become ambassadors of the change.

# Continuous improvement meetings

Ensure that your continuous improvement meetings or activities include employees from all levels. Don't allow continuous improvement groups to be only comprised of leaders. Don't fool yourself. Including employees from all levels brings subject matter expertise and brings buy-in. Continuous improvement meetings are an opportunity for inclusion.

# One-on-one exchanges

STAMP coaching sessions are a way to include the employees and leaders you supervise in a very connected way. STAMP coaching is probably the most effective way you can include employees and leaders. Coaching sessions need to happen regularly and always address the change at hand. As indicated in chapter 14, asking some of the following questions can be helpful:

✓ What do you think you might be losing/gaining as part of this change?
✓ What good things can come from this change?

✓ How could you help change the morale in our team?

✓ How can you support your colleagues?

✓ What would be the pros and cons of this solution?

✓ What are the challenges to this change? How could we address or solve these problems? How would you solve this problem? What is a better way of doing this work?

✓ How can I support you better?

✓ How can you better take care of yourself?

Again, it is critical to talk to employees individually whenever possible. It is important to know how they are feeling and know their losses. It is equally important for you to help the employee identify the hope and opportunity in the change, and empower the employee to identify solutions. Also, it is your opportunity to state your expectation of the employee regarding the change. Ensure these conversations are happening, and ensure the leaders that report to you have the necessary training, skills and commitment to having these conversations with their employees.

## Regular assessments and surveys

Checking in with employees through surveys or other feedback mechanisms is often one of the easiest ways to promote employee inclusion, and one of the most often ignored vehicles. Assessments can give you baseline information and ideas to help you, the leader, strategize opportunities. They can help you understand what is working and not working. They can help you focus on specific teams or bodies of work that need addressing. They are an opportunity that can provide rich and meaningful data. Don't miss this powerful opportunity.

# All-hands meetings

Regularly planned all-hands meetings are sometimes avoided by leaders because leaders often dread what could happen in all-staff or all-hands meetings. Leaders worry that employees will voice too many concerns or will question leadership. Issues and concerns may be raised, but the leader cannot miss the opportunity for employee inclusion simply because they are afraid or because of past experiences. Again, having structure in place for facilitating all-hands meetings helps keep meetings productive, informative and meaningful. If the leader is fearful of overwhelming negative response or dismissal, the leader can share ideas and visions and allow employees to talk about concerns for a stated time of five or ten minutes. Also, the leader can invite employees to offer concerns via email or other means but ask that each employee offer a solution as part of that concern.

Another effective strategy worth considering is asking employees to facilitate the all-hands meetings with you. Giving employees a "voice" in the change can have positive effects; often more employees give credence to the change because a colleague rather than the leader is describing the change vision or process. The colleague can be seen as more credible, and more employees will commit to the change than if only the very upper leadership is talking.

# Writing the change leadership and/or project management plan

Asking for employee help in writing the change leadership and/or project management plan is another effective way to promote employee inclusion. By including staff in the thinking and writing of the plan, employee buy-in and commitment will be dramatically increased. They will feel involved and part of the change.

Using any, many, or all of these strategies to include staff members will result in a huge return on investment for any organization. Most leaders dismiss inclusion because they believe it is too much work or it devalues their own leadership. Promoting inclusion of staff will only serve to support a positive, efficient and effective way to implement change successfully.

# Chapter 16: Building Effective Teams

Building Effective Teams addresses and alleviates losses in positive outlook, security, competence, identity, belonging, competence and trust.

## Pre-Test: How are you doing with your team?

Indicate your level of agreement using the scale **1—Strongly Disagree, 2—Disagree, 3—Agree, 4—Strongly Agree.**

1. My team knows my expectations that I have of them as a team.
2. The team has ground rules established regarding behavior.
3. I encounter individuals that poison the other team members with negativity, gossip or poor behaviors.
4. I recognize the team's good work.
5. I make sure the team celebrates accomplishments and milestones.

*Score:*

*Key:*

*19 or above –Exceptional*

*15 to 18 –Good with development opportunities*

*13-14 –Needs improvement*

*Below 13 –Need to address immediately*

Don't underestimate the power of your team. Don't underestimate how your team members can support each other during change to bring about a positive outcome. Often leaders discount the power of their teams and allow their teams to continue to be dysfunctional and nonproductive. Yes, individual employees need to be attended to, but the team members have tremendous power to address each other's losses, see opportunities and hopes, and bring morale up. Consider using the below table as a method to help a team discuss opportunities, hopes and solutions.

| Change Components | Loss? | Gain? | Challenges | Opportunities | Solutions or Actions | Support Needed for Self and through Others |
|---|---|---|---|---|---|---|
| | | | | | | |
| | | | | | | |
| | | | | | | |
| | | | | | | |

Sometimes, teams don't trust each other. Or they have had poor experiences with each other in the past. Maybe they don't really know each other. Find ways, through team-building activities, to build those relationships and work through conflict. Outside consultants administering personality-type tests or communication style inventories help employees see and value differences. Some leaders have found that developing team "charters" during change brings the team a unified and collective purpose. Charter writing does not have to take a lot of time, and usually teams can develop a charter quickly. Collective writing of charters can promote team inclusion and a sense of team purpose.

Share not only individual expectations with employees, but also group or team expectations. Acknowledge the teams and work with them to identify group ground rules and/or group norms. It is even more powerful to facilitate the team in developing ground rules and expectations during change. If the team identifies those ground rules and expectations, they will be more likely to implement them. Some of the expectations during change might include:

- Assume positive intent from the organization, leader, team and team members.
- Be honest and authentic.
- Listen to each other's concerns and issues, and provide emotional support.
- Expect that each team member will bring forward problems in a respectful and positive manner.
- Participate in problem-solving, and encourage others to problem-solve.
- Address team members' poor performance in a positive interaction.
- Stop rumor mills, and don't participate in negative and unproductive conversations.
- Support team members in providing training to each other.
- Allow mistakes and forgive others.

*Tips*

- During the next team meeting, establish some teaming ground rules.
- State your expectation that team members will support each other.
- Recognize team members and celebrate their accomplishments.
- Deal with team members' bad performances or behaviors. Don't ignore bad behavior.

If you suspect the team performance or morale is poor, address it. Don't ignore it. Use your perceptions, observations, and coaching opportunities to identify possible strategies to address poor team morale. Is one person or are two people spreading negativity through the group? Coach them, share your expectations, and hold them accountable. Do not allow them to continue with negative talk and creating a negative workplace. Is the team's poor morale due to overwhelming workloads? Review the workloads. Is there a way you can make work more equitable or more efficient? Can you help employees prioritize work? Is fun missing from the workplace? Can you figure out a way you can bring some celebratory events or appropriate fun into the work place? Are employees feeling unrecognized or not valued? Make sure you recognize employees and celebrate their good work.

Using strategies to build more cohesive teams – through the development of ground rules, expectations, recognition, celebrations and trust-building activities – will create more collaboration, increased positive outlook and morale, and ultimately higher productivity. Ignoring poor team behavior will only result in lowered morale and productivity.

# Chapter 17: Training

Training addresses and alleviates losses in identity and competence.

## Pre-Test: How is your organization doing?

Indicate your level of agreement using the scale **1—Strongly Disagree, 2—Disagree, 3—Agree, 4—Strongly Agree.**

1. Leaders have been trained in general leadership principles.
2. Leaders have participated in Privilege training.
3. Leaders have been trained in leading change.
4. Leaders have participated in 360 evaluations.
5. Poor leadership behaviors are quickly and effectively addressed.
6. Employees are trained to implement change.
7. Training plans for employees with changed job functions due to the change are in place.

*Score:*

*Key:*

*23 or above – Exceptional*

*19 to 22 – Good with development opportunities*

*16-18 – Needs improvement*

*Below 16 – Need to address immediately*

Training is often the most neglected activity during change despite its necessity. Training is needed for the leaders and the employees without direct reports. Leaders need change leadership, emotional intelligence, how to have a difficult conversation training, as well as basic managerial and leadership training. Employees without direct reports need teaming and change management training. Employees with different job requirements due to the change event may need training to address their new job functions.

Expecting supervisors, managers, directors or others who have never been trained to effectively lead to implement change is ridiculous. Allowing supervisors, managers, directors or others to continue to lead in such inappropriate styles such as micromanaging, bullying, passively allowing complacency, avoiding healthy conflict, and neglecting coaching and development activities is a disgrace.

In order to implement change effectively, it is imperative that there is strong change leadership present in all levels of supervision and management. Change leadership is a combination of leadership and management skills and functions. Leadership and management intersect, and must go hand-in-hand. An effective change leader uses Change Leadership Emotional Intelligence to manage the organizational vision and work, to inspire others, and to innovate. To implement change, the leader has to have both strong leadership skills and strong management skills. A good change leader is one who understands the importance of people and relationships and how to motivate people to do the work effectively, efficiently and where there is personal job satisfaction.

*Tips*

- Train employees to deal with change.
- Train leaders to lead change.
- Train leaders to be effective leaders.
- Address leaders who cannot lead effectively through job reassignment, intensive leadership boot camps, and 360 evaluations. Most supervisors don't know how to lead under any circumstances—in

environments with change or environments without change. Sadly, most leaders are wrongly promoted for leadership positions because they are technically talented. It is assumed that if the leader did well in the job they had, they would probably do well leading a group of people in that job area. This thinking is flawed. Good technical workers are not necessary good at leading others. Leaders need to be trained and mentored. Too often, organizations keep leaders who deal with employees or colleagues poorly. Perhaps the leader is a bully, arrogant, a tyrant or a micromanager. Instead of addressing the areas of opportunities, leaders continue to let other leaders misbehave and demonstrate poor leadership skills. They might be great managers, who can set milestones and develop project plans, but they can't lead people in a way that results in a positive return on investment.

Leaders need to be trained and mentored. They need to participate in 360 evaluations, participate in training, and be coached to be exemplary leaders. They need to use their Change Leadership Emotional Intelligence in ways that help them plan for and implement the best change management techniques and strategies. Ideally prior to the change event, leaders need to be trained on leadership basics as well as change leadership strategies. However, if a leader is noting the lack of change leadership during a change, that leader needs to participate in change leadership training. Invest wisely early to make sure the leaders are trained in change leadership and general leadership training as well as implementing a leadership coach program.

If the organization has one, several, or many leaders who are not interested in feedback, training and mentoring, it is time for the organization to be more intentional rather than ignoring the leader. For these leaders, more intensive yet participatory actions might be required, such as an intensive leadership boot camps where the leader attends and actively participates in a week or ten-day event. During these events, the leader participates in a review of 360s, meets with work coaches, engages in role play interactions, and participates in an intense training environment. Often, organizations send managers and leaders to this kind of event when the leader is bright and capable but lacks skills in dealing with people. Despite many development opportunities that are available for organizations, if a leader cannot not coach effectively, he or she should be delegated to other duties where leading others is not required.

Employees who do not supervise others need to participate in training; minimally some type of teaming and change management training. When employees understand change, the dynamics of change, and how to lead change as an individual contributor, they will be less likely to display resistance, will work through their own emotional scenarios, will be able to identify opportunities in change, and will be able to support their colleagues/leaders during change. They will be more likely to engage in behaviors needed for the change (such as positive attitude, increased productivity, and commitment to stay at the company or organization). Spending several hours with staff to participate in change training will bring a tremendous return on investment to any change event. It is worth the investment.

Finally, leaders continually need to facilitate a training skill gap assessment, to determine who needs to be trained on what due to the change event. That can be done through a simple survey, one-on-one coaching sessions, or other avenues to collect information.

# Chapter 18: Project Plans, Milestones, Accountability and Metrics

Using a project plan, identifying milestones, accountability and metrics addresses and alleviates loss areas including: positive outlook, security, leadership and support.

## Pre-Test: How is your organization doing?

Indicate your level of agreement using the scale **1—Strongly Disagree, 2—Disagree, 3—Agree, 4—Strongly Agree.**

1. Project management plans are written for "change events" that are complex in nature.
2. Employees are involved with plan writing.
3. Project management plans include milestones and timelines.
4. Project management plans are revisited and usable.
5. Project goals and accomplishments are visibly posted.

*Score:*

*Key:*

*19 or above – Exceptional*

*15 to 18 – Good with development opportunities*

*13-14 – Needs improvement*

*Below 13 – Need to address immediately*

If your change is relatively simple and uncomplicated, you may not need a project management plan. Most organizations, even when the changed process, structure, or product is fairly complex, neglect to develop a project management plan. They don't develop a plan because they aren't sure what the outcome might look like or they think it would take too much time to develop. A project management plan provides an intentional way for management to plan and think about the changes, and helps with implementation of the change. Even when leaders think a change is simple and straightforward, often it turns out to be complex with many pieces. Using a project management plan ensures that the change management plan will stay on target. Staff knows who is doing what, and the plan ensures accountability.

Project management is the activity of planning, organizing, motivating, and controlling resources and procedures to achieve goals. It is to produce a change in product, service, process, organizational structure or other outcome with a defined beginning and end. Project management plans help an organization to make change effectively. Developing a project management plan is a vital part of the overall change management plan. Importantly, developing a project management plan without an overall change management plan is a critical mistake. Project management plans are usually about what tasks need to be completed, identification of metrics and deliverables with roles and responsibilities. While a project plan is about the work that needs to get done, a change leadership plan is about the people. Organizations need a change management plan that includes the project management plan.

*Tips*

- A project management plan is needed if your change has many moving parts or complexities.
- Include employees in the writing of the plan.
- Ensure that the plan includes project scope, roles and responsibilities and resources schedules, risk management ideas, project tracking and metrics.

- Don't "shelve" the document after it is written.
- Remember to celebrate accomplishments and milestones.

The elements of a project management include:

# Project Scope

A project scope includes the objective, milestones and deliverables of the change. It includes the requirements, assumptions and constraints, as well as stakeholder analysis. The project scope provides the context and framework for leaders and staff to understand the requirements and milestones of the change. It allows the leaders and staff to consider the internal and external stakeholders' interests and needs. It provides financial or quality assumptions of the change. It helps leaders and staff get grounded in the change and why the change is needed, and it provides the general direction of what needs to happen.

# Roles, Responsibilities and Resources

With a well written project plan, roles and responsibilities of employees are listed. With a project plan, key roles of staff can be listed with responsibilities. Certainly, all employees' roles cannot be listed, but the staff performing certain tasks and staff holding others accountable should be listed. Along with roles and responsibilities, resources need to be identified: existing resources and necessary resources that are required as part of the change.

# Schedule

A time schedule listing out project timelines helps the team know whether they are on track or off track. When the schedule is available to relevant staff, employees can review the progress of the change and determine if a change in strategy is needed. Employees also feel a sense of accomplishment when they see a timeline with milestones met.

## Risk Management Plan

A thoughtful addition to a project management plan includes a risk management section. In this section, risks can be identified and then addressed with possible solutions. By thinking about risks and alternative strategies, the project planners and leaders are forced to be intentional in thinking about potential risks and understanding that they need to be agile in planning and revisions. A lack of understanding that the change (or the change implementation process) will probably evolve will only create rigidity in thinking.

## Project Tracking, Metrics

The plan needs to be tracked by not only one individual, but ideally by leaders and employees. Creating a project management plan and monitoring the plan with employees at all levels creates inclusion and buy-in. If there is just one individual – the designated project manager – assigned to evaluate the metrics and tracking of goals, then only that one individual is deeply invested in the change.

With goals and metrics, it is important that these results be posted visually to all employees. Using Gantt charts (timelines with designated outcomes) on the organizational walls creates overall organizational buy-in, encourages discussions and enhances commitment to the change.

# Chapter 19: Diagnosing and Evaluating

Diagnosing and Evaluating assesses all loss areas including positive outlook, control, competence, security, territory, belonging, trust, leadership and support.

## Pre-Test: How is your organization doing?

Indicate your level of agreement using the scale **1—Strongly Disagree, 2—Disagree, 3—Agree, 4—Strongly Agree.**

1. Surveys or other diagnostic tools are used during change events to evaluate workplace "climate".
2. Surveys or other diagnostic tools are used to evaluate leadership effectiveness.
3. Surveys or other diagnostic tools are used to evaluate changes.
4. Data from surveys are used to form leadership strategies.
5. Data survey results are shared with employees to promote inclusion.

*Score:*

*Key:*

*19 or above – Exceptional*

*15 to 18 – Good with development opportunities*

*13-14 – Needs improvement*

*Below 13 – Need to address immediately*

It is critical that leaders have the information to appropriately identify and implement strategic change roadmaps, to ensure that change is effectively being implemented and to ensure that the roadmap changes based on what the employees are doing, thinking and feeling. Most leaders will often use their own personal experiences with embracing change, or their experience in leading change, to identify appropriate strategies. However, using only this information does not usually result in a robust strategic plan. Leaders need to find out what the people in the organization are really thinking and feeling. Without the use of diagnostic tools, metrics and "check-ins," organizations are often ineffective and unsuccessful in developing effective change and communication plans. Leaders find themselves guessing and fumbling. Morale is poor, and productivity is marginal, but leaders are unsure if morale is actually better or worse. Employees may be resistant, angry and "checked out" and have a belief system that leaders don't care to find out how they are doing. Leaders are unsure of the power their own leaders carry. Are the leaders strong or are they weak? No one is sure, actually, because no one asked the employees. Bottom line, leaders have to do diagnostics. If the leader operates and makes decisions without using regular diagnostics, he or she dramatically increases the risk to the organization, employee morale, productivity, and the reputation of the leader.

*Tips*

- Establish morale and leadership baselines.
- Periodically revisit morale and leadership baselines.
- Use surveys to gain data.
- Use data to determine strategic leadership efforts.

Organizations and companies benefit from using evaluation tools and diagnostics to determine the organization's readiness for change, morale status, and the general environment of change. With diagnostics, the leader can identify needed leadership skill development, change strategies and possible training needed. Road maps can be created to plan and implement strategies that lead to positive outcomes. Using tools evaluating individual employee's perceptions along with productivity reports, helps leaders identify and implement strategies to address areas of concerns or resistance. Without this information, leadership strategies to increase employee engagement and commitment to the change may be irrelevant and ineffective.

Any survey instrument used should have integrity. The items should be carefully constructed to avoid double-barreled questions or items with double meanings and so forth. In addition, surveys should always be anonymous because, if they aren't, the leader will probably not get a true reflection on people's thoughts or feelings. Whenever possible, use an outside entity to facilitate the survey and its interpretation. The use of an outside entity promotes integrity and trust within the organization.

# Evaluation Tools

Using tools to evaluate the overall organizational health and employees' reported productivity levels helps leaders identify a comprehensive change management plan that includes relevant and effective strategies. Mistakes, areas of concern, low mood, and poor productivity can be pinpointed. Poor leadership can be identified and addressed. Using tools and diagnostics allows organizations to evaluate the success of change events. Through the use of these diagnostics the leader will enhance the likelihood of the change being implemented successfully and effectively. This will result in improved organizational health.

## *Employee Engagement Tools*

This diagnostic is used to evaluate employees' levels of engagement, commitment to the company, and general morale.

Engagement is critical because research suggests that the more that employees are engaged with the organization, the more likely productivity is high, absenteeism is low and morale is more positive. This tool should be distributed optimally prior, during, and after the change event. Highly functional organizations use this assessment tool annually at a minimum, regardless of if there are changes in the organization. See Appendix B for possible survey items.

## Change Preferences Tool

This diagnostic reveals how individuals deal with change. It reveals the various change "styles" or preferences. Knowing employees' styles allows leaders to better facilitate change. This tool helps not only the leaders, but also the employees to be reflective regarding their own personal change styles. This tool actually helps employees and leaders identify how they can implement change better. See Appendix C for possible survey items.

## Organizational Change Readiness Tool

This comprehensive diagnostic tool enables companies to evaluate all employees' perceptions of the organization, its leaders, and their readiness for change. It reveals the mood of the organization and reported productivity levels, and it produces a robust report with specific recommendations. See Appendix for D for possible survey items.

## Leadership CLEI Skills and Abilities Tool

This diagnostic evaluates the supervisors, managers, directors, and other leaders' change skills and abilities, providing recommendations to improve and enhance those skills, enabling leaders to effectively facilitate change. Based on these results, leaders can work with other leaders to develop meaningful leadership development plans that might include training, mentoring and other learning activities. See Appendix E for possible survey items.

# Chapter 20: Being Positive and Caring for Thyself

Change is tough. Change is pain for everyone. Leaders seldom take care of themselves. It is infrequent to find a leader who cares for others let alone for him or herself. Being positive and caring for thyself addresses and alleviates the leader's losses and alleviates all losses in others.

## Pre-Test: How is your organization doing?

Indicate your level of agreement using the scale 1—Strongly Disagree, 2—Disagree, 3—Agree, 4—Strongly Agree.

1. I make sure to physically exercise during change.
2. Leaders from all levels are encouraged to exercise during change.
3. Iam generally happy at work.
4. Leaders from all levels are encouraged to eat right during change.
5. I make sure to talk to a confidant during change.
6. Leaders from all levels are encouraged to talk to a confidant during change.
7. I make sure to get enough sleep during change.
8. Leaders are coached to make sure they are getting adequate rest during change.
9. I make sure to seek out additional counseling or support if needed during change.
10. Leaders from all levels are encouraged to seek out additional counseling or support if needed during change.

*Score:*

*Key:*

*38 or above – Exceptional*

*30 to 37 – Good with development opportunities*

*20 to 29 – Needs improvement*

*Below 20 – Need to address immediately*

Change is tough. Change is pain for everyone. Leaders seldom take care of themselves. It is infrequent to find a leader who cares for others let alone for him or herself.

According to neuroscientists, when people hear of change, they feel pain. A leader who is effective at leading should be exhausted leading all those employees with pain. It is exhausting to lead change effectively. Leading change without considering change management principles is less arduous than leading change with the people in mind. Leaders who want to lead a successful change management event must be taking care of themselves. Whether that is exercise, finding a confidant, meditation, eating right and sleeping well, leaders needs to take care of themselves first.

*Tips*

- Exercise.
- Find a positive confidant.
- Meditate.
- Eat right.
- Sleep.
- Reach out for counseling support if needed.

## *Exercise*

During change, leaders usually don't have time. They are busy with meetings, dealing with issues, and working longer hours. They find themselves not having quality time at home and usually have given up on their exercise regime... if they even had one. Making the time to exercise will help leaders gain insight to problems, see issues with more clarity, elevate their mood, manage stress and help them to be in better physical shape. Even if the leader can be involved in brief exercise, he or she will be better equipped to deal with the change and the challenges that change can bring. The busy leader might want to consider:

- A fifteen-minute walk at lunch.
- Participating in a weekly yoga class.
- 20 minutes in the gym.

## *Find a Confidant*

Finding a confidant outside of the workplace is a positive and healthy strategy. Usually leaders find someone internal to the organization, but meeting and talking continuously about work problems can spread negative emotional contagion. Also, an external confidant can provide an objective perspective to the issues the leader is addressing. It is important to note, however, that you should choose a confidant who is not always negative and with a tendency to see the glass "half empty". Given how emotional contagion plays out, you need to be intentional that your confidant doesn't pollute you with their negative emotional responses.

When meeting with your confidant, make sure you give them context for healthy interactions. Ask that they listen, and ask that they help you see the opportunities in your situation. Choosing a confidant who is typically negative in interactions is not helpful to you. Perhaps you can identify someone who is a good listener, someone who is positive, and yet will give you honest feedback.

## Meditate

Using mindfulness and other med helps leaders techniques help their minds and remain focused at work. Whether you take a class, participate in a taped guided meditation, or implement a meditation strategy of your own, you will likely find yourself to be calmer, more in control of the emotions you are experiencing and overall better equipped to handle work situations and problems.

## Eat Right

During change, leaders usually don't eat right; in fact, they tend to eat more junk food and fewer regular meals because they are stressed out. Let's face it—if you eat garbage, do you really feel confident, positive and good about yourself? Probably not. Choosing foods that are healthier in nature, using appropriate portion size, and avoiding food choices that make one wired or crabby will result in a leader having a more positive attitude and well-being.

## Sleep Right

During change, leaders usually don't sleep as much as they need to because they are stressed out, worried, or working long hours. When leaders don't sleep, they are not at their best to deal with their own emotional responses, others' emotional responses, or problems that present in the day. If you are someone who doesn't sleep well, contact your doctor. It is becoming increasing clear that we need to sleep. We need to sleep to properly store memories, regulate our feelings and emotions, and rid our bodies of brain cell waste. Getting enough sleep is imperative for the great leader to lead regardless whether or not there is change.

## Be Positive and Happy

Spread positivity at the workplace and with the people you lead! In Shawn Achor's book *The Happiness Advantage* [18], he speaks about the recent discoveries in the field of positive psychology. Contrary to the notion that success fuels happiness, he reports that happiness actually promotes success. He purports that the happier we are at work, the more we can transmit positivity to those we work with and lead. He goes on to say "Studies have found that when leaders are in a positive mood, their employees are more likely to be in a positive mood themselves, to exhibit prosocial helping behaviors toward one another, and to coordinate tasks more efficiently and less effort." (p. 209).

## Employee Advisory Services or Counseling Support

Sometimes a significant change to the organization or to the leader is overwhelming. Even though the leader has attempted to cope with the change, for some reason he or she cannot embrace it. For situations where the change is insurmountable, leaders – along with any employees who are experiencing this – should consider other external support. Perhaps the organization has an Employee Advisory Program (EAP) or an Employee Advisory Service (EAS) where one can participate in counseling support. If the organization does not have an EAP program, the employee can participate in some counseling sessions external to the company. The bottom line is that employees and leaders need to care for themselves and get the support they need.

# Section 4:  Putting It All Together: CLEI

Section 1 of this book discussed kinds of change, common mistakes, and understanding change losses.  Section 2 specifically addressed how to think about leading change within an emotional intelligence framework, and Section 3 described the techniques and tools that may be found in the change leadership toolbox. Now in this Section 4 we put it all together by considering the importance of using a change management written road map along with the importance of an organization remaining fluid and nimble.

# Chapter 21: Writing the Change Management Plan or the Change Roadmap

Leaders are more often interested in project management plans than leadership plans. Those leaders who write only a project plan are asking for failure. Certainly, they will have the giant charts, timelines, milestones and people responsible, yet the project management plan doesn't motivate people to do their work. No one is coaching the followers. No one is coaching the supervisors. These leaders focus only on outcomes, falsely believing that stating goals and activities will serve as a motivational tool for everyone.

*In Appendix F, my colleague Kevin Whitley provides a great visual of a change management plan and project management plan combined.*

An appropriate change management plan includes a well-written and well-thought-out project management plan, but it also includes the critical Change Leadership Emotional Intelligence (CLEI) functions. The change leadership plan includes change management strategies. However the plan is written – completing a table, writing a narrative, etc. – the plan needs to be executed.

See below for a list of essential change leadership pieces, with questions to ask your organization and a column to make comments.

| Strategy or Action | Questions to Ask or Issues to Include | Comments and Status |
|---|---|---|
| Visioning | Does the vision or purpose statement include essential elements: The "what" The "why" The "how" The "hope" | |

|  | The role of employees | |
|---|---|---|
|  | Acknowledgement of emotions | |
|  | Call for commitment | |
|  | At what frequency will the vision/purpose statement be stated? And how? | |
| Role "Fitting" | What are static and changing roles of employees? | |
|  | Have role "fitting" discussions occurred? | |
|  | Have road-mapping conversations happened? | |
| Communicating | Is communication happening: | |
|  | Kick-off planned? | |
|  | Emails being sent? | |
|  | All staff meetings scheduled? | |
|  | Coaching sessions being facilitated? | |
|  | Team discussions planned? | |
|  | Does messaging include: | |
|  | Vision or purpose? | |
|  | Details of change? | |
|  | Role descriptions? | |
|  | Challenges and possible problem-solving opportunities? | |
|  | Hope, opportunity and reassurance? | |
|  | Invitation for more conversation? | |
| Motivating, Recognizing or Celebrating | What are plans to recognize: | |
|  | Individuals? | |
|  | Teams? | |
|  | Larger groups and organization? | |
|  | What celebration events are planned? | |
| STAMP Coaching | What are the expectations and accountability measures to ensure leaders coach employees? | |
|  | What are the expectations and accountability measures to ensure that leaders coach supervisors, | |

| | | |
|---|---|---|
| | managers and other leaders? When will the leaders be trained to effectively coach using STAMP? | |
| Facilitating Inclusion | What types of communication have been planned: Regular and ongoing communication? Focus groups? Staff or team meetings? What types of inclusionary methods are being used: Planning meetings? Continuous improvement meetings? All-hands meetings? Individual exchanges? | |
| Building Effective Teams | Does the team know change support expectations? Is the team functional or does the team needs to participate in team building activities? Is there a plan to celebrate the teams? | |
| Training | What change management training has been delivered to: All employees? Leaders? What specific or technical training needs to be provided to employees with role changes or task changes? How will this be evaluated? Have leaders been trained to be leaders? | |
| Project Plan Development | Is there a plan with: A detailed project scope that includes objectives and deliverables, requirements, assumptions and constraints, and stakeholder analysis? Roles, responsibilities and resources delineated? A time schedule or timeline described? A discussion regarding risks and possible alternative | |

| | | |
|---|---|---|
| | strategies? | |
| | Metrics and milestones listed to allow for monitoring and tracking? | |
| Diagnosing and Evaluating | When will an Employee Engagement survey be administered? Re-administered? How will results be used? | |
| | Will a change preference survey be used? If so, when? How will results be used? | |
| | When will the Organizational Change Readiness survey be implemented? How will results be used? | |
| | When will a Leadership CLEI Skills and Abilities instrument are used? How will results be used? | |
| Being Positive and Caring for Oneself | What are your plans and your leaders' plans to: | |
| | Exercise? | |
| | Get needed support? | |
| | Other activities that alleviate stress | |

# Chapter 22: Sustaining Change and Remaining Fluid

Sustaining change maybe difficult for an organization. It may be that employees or leaders are resisting the change and behave in a manner to sabotage the change. Many employees often revert to the old way of doing business because management or leaders are simply not holding employees accountable, nor are the leaders paying attention to the change. Continued attention to a change is critical. How can that attention be manifested? Attention can be manifested through visual metrics, continued conversations, accolades and recognition of change.

As important as it is to sustain change, leaders must be cognizant of their role to create a fluid work environment where continuous change is accepted, embraced and desired. Many leaders try to comfort employees by saying things like "We are almost done", "Soon this change will be implemented and won't have to change again" or "We have to stop changing things around here". Comments like those convey that the organization will soon experience status quo. But, by accepting this assumption, the organization will probably not thrive or stay competitive. Organizations that create a culture of fluidity will create an organization that is alive and vibrant.

So, as important as it is to sustain the changed process, product, location or whatever the change might be, it is equally important for employees and leaders at all levels to understand that change and ongoing change is vital to all organizations. Change leadership skills are critical to successful leaders. Change skills for all employees are necessary. Understanding the importance and need for change is a fundamental tenet for successful organizations. Instead of leaders offering comments that indicate the change is almost over, the leader needs to be offering comments that indicate how good it is that the organization is comprised at all levels of change agents. The leader should praise the employees and leaders for the successful change implementation, tell them why change is important and share confidence that ongoing change will be implemented successfully. Most importantly, leaders at every level must be held accountable for practicing CLEI, and for using effective change strategies—specifically STAMP coaching principles. With this approach, the leader has set the table for a living and changing organization.

# Conclusion

Implementing successful change is harder than it may at first appear. An exemplary change leader must understand the importance of Change Leadership Emotional Intelligence. The leader must understand the use of CLEI concepts to effectively inform how to lead change effectively. The leader needs to understand how they feel about the change, to have a handle on their own emotional responses, and must be able to empathize with others during change. They need to explore employees' losses so that they can help those employees see the hope and opportunities in change through effective STAMP coaching methods. The leader must ensure that all employees are included in change formulation, implementation and evaluation. Understanding the importance of CLEI and the use of effective change strategies will enhance the likelihood of effective change implementation.

# Appendices

# Appendix A: Role Mapping Exercise

1.  Ask employees to bring a list of their work activities that are a part of the new change event. You may want to spend time in preparation for this exercise by coaching employees to identify their work activities and tasks. You want to spend time especially with employees who may be struggling or are unable to identify anticipated work activities. Be prepared to think through how each employee's role supports the change. Even if individuals' job tasks don't support the change directly, make sure that indirect linkages will be made, such as a confidential secretary's or security personnel.

2.  Post the organization's vision on a wall. Post the change strategic vision under the vision, showing how the change vision supports the organization's vision. Then post the change components or major outputs under the change vision. Ask the employees to write their job tasks down on post-its. Ask the employees to walk to the wall and post their post-it under the change component which that particular activity supports. Ask the employees to use yarn or string to indicate how that particular activity supports the change effort and the organizational vision. Then, use a different colored string to identify linkages or supports to other employees.

3.  Review the "collage" of visions, components and linkages. Add to the wall. Add change components and job tasks. Take a picture of the wall so you can use this visual diagram to help employees to further identify their role, development needs, and for further discussion.

# Appendix B: Employee Engagement Diagnostic

Indicate your level of agreement using the scale 1—**Strongly Disagree,** 2—**Disagree,** 3—**Agree,** 4—**Strongly Agree.**

1. I have at least one real work "friend".
2. I enjoy my work.
3. I am proud of the work I do.
4. I am proud of the organization where I work.
5. I know how I fit into this organization.
6. I bring value to this organization.
7. I generally enjoy my team.
8. I generally enjoy my supervisor.
9. I generally enjoy my colleagues.
10. I plan to stay at this organization.
11. I care about the quality of work I perform.
12. I care about how efficiently I do my work.
13. I am enthusiastic about my job.
14. I give my "all" to the job.
15. I want to help others when they need help.
16. I offer to do more work whenever I am able.
17. I look forward to going to work.
18. I feel positive about my work.
19. I have a great relationship with my boss.
20. I would recommend this organization as a great place to work.

*Scoring:*
*70- 80: High level engagement*
*59- 69: Engagement*
*58 or below:Lack of engagement*

Additional questions to ask:

1. I am not likely to work at my highest level.
2. I sometimes sabotage my work or others' work.
3. I am embarrassed to work at this organization.
4. I intend on seeking alternative work quickly.

# Appendix C: Change Preferences Survey

Choose only one answer for each question that best fits you:

1. Regarding implementing change at work...
   a. I like to experiment and implement ideas even though the change has not been "thought out".
   b. I only like to implement ideas after understanding the rationale for the change and how it fits together.
   c. I don't like to take risks at work because the change isn't worth the problems associated with it.
   d. I plan to implement any change once the directive is given.

2. When I listen to the new change "vision" or "big picture"...
   a. My immediate reaction is excitement.
   b. I am bored with the presentation.
   c. I want to hear about why the change is being considered.
   d. I get nervous that it will actually happen.

3. When hearing about the change project...
   a. I get worried about implementing the change if the details haven't been thought out and identified.
   b. I am neutral about the changes being discussed and will implement the change when it happens.
   c. I am depressed and hope the change will never be implemented.
   d. I am excited to think of an "out of the box" solution and want to try it.

4. When there is a change at work I think I might not like...
   a. I will just go along with it once I am told what I am supposed to do.

b. I will ask a lot of questions about why it is happening, and identify issues that need to be resolved.

c. I try to avoid the change and hope I don't have to implement it.

d. I will try it out without many reservations.

5. A phrase that best describes how I think about change is...
   a. "I hate to question you, but why are we doing this?"
   b. "If it's not broke, don't fix it".
   c. "Tell me what to do and I will do it".
   d. "Variety is the spice of life".

6. When there is change at work...
   a. I like to work with the same group of people that I am familiar with.
   b. I like to work with new people that I don't know very well.
   c. I like to work with the people the organization thinks makes a good team.
   d. I like to work with people where I know what skill each brings to the table.

7. Often I think of myself as...
   a. A dreamer.
   b. A practical person.
   c. Someone who likes routine.
   d. Someone who does what I am told.

8. When change doesn't work out...
   a. I identify all the pain points or problems.
   b. I think of other experiments or ideas to try.
   c. I just hope that things can go back to the "old way".

d. I realize that I will be told to do something differently.

*Scoring:*

*Assign one of the following letter combinations to each question according to whether you answered a, b, c or d.*

1. a. SCA
   b. AT
   c. P
   d. C

2. a. SCA
   b. C
   c. AT
   d. P

3. a. AT
   b. C
   c. P
   d. SCA

4. a. C
   b. AT
   c. P
   d. SCA

5. a. AT
   b. P
   c. C
   d. SCA

6.  a. P
    b. SCA
    c. C
    d.AT

7.  a. SCA
    b.AT
    c. P
    d. C

8.  a. AT
    b. SCA
    c. P
    d. C

*Now calculate the total for each let combination:*

*SCA Score:*
*AT Score:*
*C Score:*
*P Score:*

Those letter combinations represent your change preferences as described next.

# Change Preferences – What Do They Mean?

**Super Change Agents (SCA)**...are people that for the most part like change. They welcome change. They dream of changes. If they get bored, they will often make changes. Sometimes the change is not quite thought out and may be presented in abstract terms. SCAs bring value to change. The SCAs bring "dreaming" and "visioning" to organizations and sometimes need help in working out the strategy/details. Be careful not to dismiss their ideas and enthusiasm.

**Activist/Theorists (AT)**...are people that for the most part like change once they feel like the change have been justified. They ask questions and are sometimes skeptical of change. After careful consideration, they often embrace the change. The ATs bring value to change. They can identify potential barriers or challenges that the change might bring. They can help "flush" out ideas. Sometimes they need help in expressing vision and encouragement to be enthusiastic about the change. Be careful not to dismiss their questions and inquiries. Encourage and reassure them.

**Compliants (C)**...are people that for the most part will embrace change once the details are known and they know what they are supposed to do. They typically don't value the "visioning" exercises or the sessions where ideas are "fleshed out". They will participate but will be paying attention to the actual new tasks, processes, or other details. C's bring value to change. They feel positive about change once they know what the change entails. Sometimes they need reassurance that even though the details of the change are not known yet, those details will be known soon. Be careful not to dismiss these peoplesimply because they aren't overly interested in visioning or working through details.

**Predictables (P)**...are people that for the most part don't seek out change nor embrace it. They enjoy patterns and routines and often are heard to say "if it isn't broke, don't fix it". They are sometimes frustrated with, and worried about, visioning and/or strategy building exercises. Sometimes they need to hear that the change is really going to happen and need to know the expectations of them. Otherwise, they might "hold out", hoping that the change will not actually occur. These individuals bring value in that once the change is made, they will perform the work without getting bored. Be careful to not stereotype them or label them as "resistors".

# Appendix D: Organizational Readiness Tool

Indicate your level of agreement using the scale **1—Strongly Disagree, 2—Disagree, 3—Agree, 4—Strongly Agree.**

1. I understand the link between what I do and organizational objectives.
2. I have a good understanding of what my organization is trying to accomplish.
3. I have been trained well to do my job.
4. If I have additional or new job responsibilities, I am trained properly.
5. My supervisor is a good leader.
6. When needed, my supervisor helps me to develop the confidence in my ability to do my job well.
7. My supervisor recognizes the good work I accomplish.
8. My supervisor talks about development opportunities with me.
9. My supervisor understands what I need to do in order to do my job effectively.
10. I trust my supervisor.
11. My supervisor cares about me as a person.
12. My supervisor values my opinion.
13. My supervisor is generally happy.
14. My supervisor listens to how I feel about situations or concerns.
15. My supervisor communicates with me well.
16. My supervisor empowers me to find solutions to job challenges.
17. In the past, when there has been change, it has been successful.
18. My supervisor helps me "connect the dots" when there is change.
19. For the most part, my team works well together.
20. During stressful times, my team members support each other.
21. I have been trained to implement change effectively.

22. During change, my supervisor explains the change.
23. During change, my supervisor encourages me to take care of myself.
24. During change, my supervisor explains how my job role fits in with the change.
25. During change, I am involved in some of the decision-making about change.
26. During change, I am empowered to think of solutions to challenges.
27. During change, I encourage my peers to adopt the change.
28. During change, I help others with their job tasks.
29. During change, I am open to changes in my job or job role.
30. During change, I try to see the positives.
31. During change, I feel good about talking with my supervisor about my concerns.

*Key:*

*90-124: Excellent readiness for change.*

*78-89: Good readiness for change with some opportunities to prepare.*

*61-77: Adequate readiness for change with many opportunities andinterventions to prepare.*

*60 or below: Organization would strongly benefit with aggressive change preparation strategies: training, consultation and intervention.*

Additional items to consider independently

32. During change, I am overly stressed.
33. During change, I am overly depressed.
34. During change, I am overly anxious.

35. During change, I am generally happy.

36. During change, I am generally energized.

37. During change I am generally fun to be with.

# Appendix E: Leadership CLEI Skills and Abilities Tool

Indicate your level of agreement using the scale 1—Strongly Disagree, 2—Disagree, 3—Agree, 4—Strongly Agree.

1. I am aware of my emotional feelings about a particular change.
2. I am able to contain my negative feelings and responses about the change when talking with others.
3. I am able to coach employees to see the hope and opportunity of change events.
4. I am able to empathize with employees regarding their feelings and thoughts about change.
5. I am able to help employees move forward in successful implementation of change.
6. The organization or I have written a "change event" vision statement.
7. I share the "change event" vision statement frequently.
8. Each employee knows how their role supports the change event.
9. Employees' roles are discussed during coaching sessions.
10. I tend to communicate the "change event" vision and details sooner rather than later.
11. Many modalities of communication are used to talk about the change vision, process and other information; e.g. email, newsletter, all-hands meetings, one-on-one coaching, and visual presentations.
12. Employees are enlisted to communicate the change vision, process and other information.
13. Change "kick-offs" are frequently used to describe changes.
14. My group celebrates what has happened in the past before it celebrates the new.
15. My group intentionally celebrates most change milestones.

16. I acknowledge employees' good performance and change behavior.

17. I provide recognition and praise often.

18. I empower employees rather than micromanage employees whenever possible.

19. I involve employees during change planning meetings.

20. I routinely communicate updates and progress regarding the change event.

21. Employees are asked for their opinions and ideas, and are encouraged to participate in change event dialogues.

22. Employees are asked to identify challenges and possible solutions during change.

23. My team knows the expectations that I have of them as a team.

24. My team is functional.

25. My team gets along with each other.

26. I challenge individuals that poison the other team members with negativity, gossip or poor behaviors.

27. I have been trained in general leadership principles.

28. I have been trained in leading change.

29. Employees are trained regarding how to implement change.

30. Surveys or other diagnostic tools are used during change events to evaluate workplace "climate".

31. Surveys or other diagnostic tools are used to evaluate my leadership effectiveness.

32. Surveys or other diagnostic tools are used to evaluate changes.

33. I make sure to physically exercise during change.

34. I make sure to eat right during change.

35. If I am struggling with change, I make sure to talk to a confidant (other than my staff) during change.

36. I make sure to get enough sleep during change.

*Key*

*108 – 144: Excellent change leadership skills*

*85-107: Good change leadership skills*

*84 or below: Needs development in overall leadership and change leadership strategies and behaviors.*

# Appendix F: Combined Change Management Plan and Project Plan

In this appendix, my colleague Kevin Whitley provides a great visual of a change management plan and project management plan combined. The infographic is shown on the following two pages.

# ABC Inc.

Where are we going...
A new system integration has a people side and a project side. Below is a high-level plan for how we will get through implementation successfully.

## Change Management

## Project Management

**STEP 01**

### Define Change Management Vision

Identify the elements needed to help stakeholders be successful.

### Requirements

- The Project Team engages subject matter experts and gathers all information needed through extensive baseline process mapping to define our requirements.
- File clean-up is initiated.

### Stakeholder Engagement and Communication

To achieve buy-in for the system implementation:

- Project Sponsor communicates the goals of the project, including roles, process changes, policy changes, and address questions and concerns.
- Initiate Ambassador Program to be a conduit of communication between locations and the project.
- Facilitated assessment, comp levels, and leadership effectiveness.
- Involving the right people in the design and plan for implementation of the new system.
- Training to better work together as a team and establish workplace norms.
- Ensure STAMP Coaching

**STEP 02**

### Selection and Procurement

Requirements are compiled and put out in a Request for Proposal. Vendors are scored, vetted, reference checked, negotiations occur, and a contract is signed.

### Development

- Implementation planning is initiated.
- Business rules are developed.
- Staffing model defined.
- LEAN process mapping conducted.
- Detailed configurations are gathered.
- Beta release is completed.
- Finish case clean-up.

**STEP 03**

### Readiness

- Getting people ready for the changes by ensuring they have the right information and tools.
- Assessing user skills.
- Conducting gap analysis.

### Integration and Testing

- Begin integration and data migration.
- System testing until accepted.

**STEP 04**

### Training

- Provide training pertinent to the needs of each user at the pilot location.

### Pilot Location Implementation

- Pilot implementation at one location.
- Develop user manuals.
- Provide user training.

### Communication

- Predict and prepare stakeholders for who, what when, where, and how.
- Discuss available support.

**STEP 05**

## Support

- Check in with Pilot stakeholders to discuss what is/is not going well.

## Demonstrations

- Maximize access to pilot court for stakeholders to see/touch /interact with new system in action.
- Opportunities to shadow those in their specific role.

## Communication

- Predict and prepare stake holders for who, what when, where, and how.
- Discuss available support.

## Feedback Loop

- Provide central place for all stakeholders to provide feedback to the project team.
- Communicate issues and status of resolutions.
- Ensure STAMP Coaching.

## Support

- Check in with stakeholders to discuss what is/is not going well.

## Empowerment

- Empower stakeholders to identify areas of "waste" and initiate LEAN Processes.
- Establish LEAN Specialist in locations.

## Support

- Build a network to raise issues within locations and courtwide.
- Facilitated assessment, comp levels, and leadership effectiveness.

## Pilot Demonstrations

**STEP 06**

Expose staff to the new system and the Pilot location will help others learn the new system.

## Refining the New System

**STEP 07**

As issues arise, are identified, the system will be refined, tested, and re-implemented.

## Full Implementation

- Implement new system.
- User manuals distributed and updated as needed.

**STEP 08**

## Refining the System

As issues arise, are identified, in the system, it will be refined, tested, and re-implemented.

## Continued Improvements

**STEP 09**

Continuous iterations of improvements and fixes will occur consistently for the first year.

## Develop Support Team

Build and maintain support for all users through training, product improvements, and system updates.

**STEP 10**

# Bibliography

[1] D. Goleman, "Working with Emotional Intelligence", New York: Bantam Books, 1998.

[2] P. B. Vaill, "Learning as a Way of Being", San Francisco: Jossey-Bass, 1996.

[3] P. Salovey and J. D. Mayer, "Emotional Intelligence.," *Imagination, Cognition, and Personality,* vol. 9, no. 3, pp. 185-211, 1990.

[4] D. Rock, "Managing with the Brain in Mind," *Strategy+Business,* no. 56, 2009.

[5] D. Rock, L. Rock, L. Davachi and T. Kiefer, "Learning that lasts through AGES," *NeuroLeadership Journal,* no. 3, 2010.

[6] E. W. Morrison and F. J. Milliken, "Organizational Silence: A Barrier to Change and Development in a Pluralistic World," *Academy of Management Review,* vol. 25, no. 4, pp. 706-725, 2000.

[7] C. J. Nemeth, "Managing Innovation: When Less is More," *California Management Review,* vol. 40, no. 1, pp. 59-74, 1997.

[8] K. Ryan and D. K. Oestreich, Driving Fear Out Of The Workplace: How to Overcome the Invisible Barriers to Quality, Productivity, and Innovation, Jossey-Bass, 1991.

[9] W. Bridges, "Transitions: Making Sense of Life's Changes", Cambridge, MA: Perseus, 2004.

[10] T. Kiefer, "Understanding the Emotional Experience of Organizational Change: Evidence from a Merger," *Advances in Developing Human Resources,* vol. 4, no. 1, pp. 39-61, 2002.

[11] D. Rock and J. Schwartz, "The Neuroscience of Leadership: Breakthroughs in brain research explain how to make organizational transformation succeed," *Strategy+Business,* no. 43, 2006.

[12] C. D. J. D. T. Scott, Managing Change at Work: Leading People Through Organizational Transitions, Menlo Park: Crisp Publications, 1995.

[13] C. J. Schaeffer, "Downsized Survivors: Areas of Loss and Work," *Dissertations and Theses,* vol. Paper 111, 2012.

[14] K. K. Goldsworthy, "Grief and loss theory in social work practice: all changes involve loss, just as all losses require change," *Australian Social Work,* vol. 58, no. 2, pp. 167-178, 2005.

[15] J. A. Murray, "Loss as a universal concept: Review of the literature to identify common aspects of loss in diverse situations," *Journal of Loss and Trauma: International Perspectives on Stress & Coping,* vol. 6, no. 3, pp. 219-241, 2001.

[16] R. A. Neimeyer, Lessons of Loss: A Guide to Coping, Memphis, TN: University of Memphis, 2000.

[17] R. Stuart, "The research context and change triggers," *Personnel Review,* vol. 24, no. 2, pp. 3-88, 1995.

[18] S. Achor, The Happiness Advantage: The Seven Principles of

Positive Psychology That Fuel Success and Performance at Work, New York: Crown Business, 2010.

[19] R. Boyatzis, "Neuroscience and the link Between Inspirational Leadership and Resonant Relationships," *Ivey Business Journal*, vol. January/February, 2012.

[20] C. Argyris and D. A. Schon, Organizational Learning: A Theory of Action Perspective, Readings, MA: Addison-Wesley, 1998.

[21] B. Nelson, 1501 Ways to Reward Employees, New York: Workman, 2012.

[22] T. M. I.-. C. V. D. a. Mihal, "The Human Science of Giving Recognition: Creating True Connections Between Humans in the Workforce," Maritz Institute- White paper, 2011.

[23] S. R. Brown, "A Match Made in Heaven: A Marginalized Methodology for Studying the Marginalized," *Quality and Quantity*, vol. 40, no. 3, pp. 361-382, 2006.

[24] S. M. Nkomo and E. L. J. Edmondson Bell, Our Separate Ways: Black and White Women and the Struggle for Professional Identity, Boston, MA: Harvard Business School Press, 2003.

[25] N. Yuval-Davis, "Belonging and the Politics of Belonging," *Patterns of Prejudice*, vol. 40, no. 3, pp. 197-214, 2006.

[26] P. McIntosh, "White privilege and Male Privilege: A Personal Account of Coming to See Correspondences through Work in Women Studies," Wellesley Centers for Women, MA, 1988.

Cyndi Schaeffer

THIS PAGE IS INTENTIONALLY BLANK

24806221R00117

Made in the USA
San Bernardino, CA
07 October 2015